ANTI-INFLAMMATORY COOKBOOK FOR BEGINNERS 2024 EDITION

Simple and Tasty Recipes to Fight Inflammatory Processes and Oxidative Stress

30 Days meal-Plan

Wilhelmine P. Blake

Table of Contents

INTRODUCTION — 6
- WHAT IS THE INFLAMMATORY PROCESS, AND WHY CAN IT BE DANGEROUS?......6
- DISEASES THAT CAN CAUSE IT......6
- WHY IS CHRONIC INFLAMMATION SO DANGEROUS, AND HOW CAN IT BE ELIMINATED?......7
- THE ROLE OF DIET......8
- CHARACTERISTICS OF AN ANTI-INFLAMMATORY DIET......8

BREAKFAST RECIPES — 9
- BANANA OATMEAL MUFFINS......9
- BLUEBERRY CHIA PUDDING......9
- OATMEAL WITH BERRIES......10
- OATMEAL COOKIES AND NUTS......10
- PUMPKIN AND OATMEAL PANCAKES......11
- OATMEAL AND APPLE COOKIES......11
- OMELET WITH EGGPLANT......12
- COCONUT AND HEMP BARS......12
- CHIA PUDDING WITH COCONUT AND TURMERIC...13
- PORRIDGE WITH GOLDEN MILK......13
- FLUFFY ARTICHOKE FRITTATA......14
- GRANOLA BOWL......14
- ACAI BOWL WITH CHOCOLATE......15
- MINI PEAR CRUMBLE WITH WALNUTS......15
- OATMEAL AND COCOA PORRIDGE......16

MAIN DISH RECIPES — 17
- WARM SALAD WITH PINE NUTS, TOMATO, AND BASIL......17
- CASSEROLE WITH CABBAGE......18
- MUSHROOM PAN WITH SPINACH......18
- MUSHROOM AND ZUCCHINI SPAGHETTI......19
- BUCKWHEAT TIMBALE, PEAS, AND TOMATO WITH SPROUTS......20
- TORTELLINI BROCCOLI CASSEROLE......21
- CASSEROLE WITH KOHLRABI......22
- CHILI CON TOFU......23
- CAULIFLOWER POTATO CURRY......24
- POKE BOWL......25
- VEGETABLE CAKES......25
- ZUCCHINI-SPAGHETTI......26
- ZUCCHINI LASAGNA......27
- VEGETARIAN MEATBALLS......28
- SAUSAGE GOULASH AND MINCED MEAT......29
- TUSCANY MEATBALLS......30
- CAULIFLOWER STEAKS WITH LENTILS......31
- CURRIED CHICKEN STRIPS......32
- OVEN GNOCCHI IN A TOMATO AND PEPPER SAUCE......32
- STUFFED CELERY WITH CHEESE......33
- APRICOT BREAD WITH CREAM CHEESE......33
- PAPRIKA RICE PAN WITH YOGURT SAUCE......34
- BRITTA'S ROBBER MEAT......35
- FETA CHEESE ON CAULIFLOWER RICE......36
- CAULIFLOWER STEAKS WITH LENTILS......37
- STUFFED SALMON TROUT FILLETS......38
- VEGETARIAN CHICKPEA CURRY WITH APRICOTS...39
- SALMON FILLET WITH PEPPERS......40
- TROUT FILLETS......41
- TOMATO SALMON......42
- OVEN VEGETABLES......43
- LEMONY FISH FILLET WITH ZUCCHINI VEGETABLES......44
- RUTABAGA AND MASHED POTATOES......45
- STEWED CUCUMBERS WITH SALMON AND DILL......46
- POTATO CHICKEN BREAST......47
- MARINATED TOFU......48
- ORANGE SALMON WITH NUT RICE......49
- SALMON SPINACH PASTA......49
- SESAME-CRUSTED SALMON AND BROCCOLI......50
- SALMON MEATBALLS ON LEEKS......51
- TARTE FLAMBEE WITH BEETROOT......52
- TAGLIATELLE AND MARINATED SALMON......53
- SALMON SPINACH ROLLS......54
- SESAME-CRUSTED SALMON AND BROCCOLI......55

SALMON WITH BEANS, TOMATOES, AND VEGETABLES..................................56
MACKEREL FILLETS..........................57
AVOCADO, ZUCCHINI, AND CHICKPEA HUMMUS....57
OATMEAL CHEESE PATTIES.......................58
HERB OMELET WITH SMOKED SALMON..................58

RECIPES FOR CAKES 59
BANANA, COCONUT, AND CHOCOLATE CAKE........59
CRANBERRY MUFFINS............................59
BEAN BROWNIE.................................60
COCONUT CAKE.................................60
CHRISTMAS GINGERBREAD........................61
BANANA WAFFLES...............................61
OATMEAL CAKE IN BLENDER......................62
EXTRA JUICY YOGURT CAKE......................63
ALMOND CAKE..................................64
COCONUT CHOCOLATE CAKE.......................65
LEMON CAKE...................................66
PLUM CAKE....................................67
APPLE CAKE...................................67
BROCCOLI AND SALMON CAKE.....................68

SNACK RECIPES 69
BANANA OATMEAL MUFFINS.......................69
TOAST WITH CHICKPEA PASTE, AVOCADO, AND TOMATOES....................................70
LENTIL RAGOUT WITH VEGETABLES................71
TURKEY THIGH WITH MUSHROOMS..................72
CARAMELIZED PEARS IN YOGURT..................73
ROASTED NUTS.................................73
ENERGY BITES.................................74
CHIA SEED PUDDING............................74
CINNAMON PARFAIT.............................75
VEGAN BLUEBERRY PIE..........................75
ZUCCHINI FETA SKEWERS........................76
ANTI-AGING WEAPON WITH RASPBERRIES...........76
ANTIOXIDANT-RICH CHOCOLATE SMOOTHIE BOWL 77
BANANA BREAD WITH CHIA SEEDS AND ALMOND MILK...77
STRAWBERRY COLLAGEN GUMS.....................78

BEVERAGE RECIPES 79
PAPAYA SMOOTHIE..............................79
GINGER TEA...................................79
SLOE JUICE...................................80
ICE-MATCHA...................................80
COLD ROSEHIP AND RASPBERRY DRINK.............81
CRANBERRY JUICE..............................81
WHEATGRASS AND PINEAPPLE SHOT................81
FLAXSEED AND DANDELION SMOOTHIE..............82
SMOOTHIE "GOLDEN MILK."......................82
COOKIES & CREAM KEFIR SHAKE..................82

SALAD RECIPES 83
CHARD SALAD..................................83
SAUERKRAUT SALAD.............................84
ARUGULA SALAD................................85
WHITE CABBAGE SALAD..........................86
KALE SALAD...................................87
SPANISH SALAD................................88
SALAD WITH HONEY MUSHROOMS...................89
SPROUT SPINACH SALAD WITH BEETROOT...........90
SUPERFOOD SUPER SALAD........................91

SIDE DISH 92
CREAM OF ASPARAGUS...........................92
STUFFED PINEAPPLE............................93
ARUGULA PESTO................................93
PEAR CHUTNEY.................................94
KKAKDUGI: RADISH KIMCHI......................94

MEAL PLANNING TIPS AND TRICKS 95
LEARN HOW TO READ NUTRITION LABELS...........95
HOW TO PLAN MEALS IN ADVANCE.................95
HOW TO MAKE HEALTHY FOOD CHOICES WHEN EATING OUT..................................96
SHOPPING LIST................................97
DAIRY ALTERNATIVES:..........................98
SUBSTITUTIONS:...............................98

30- DAYS MEAL PLAN 99
CONCLUSION 102
AN IMPORTANT REQUEST 103

INTRODUCTION

WHAT IS THE INFLAMMATORY PROCESS, AND WHY CAN IT BE DANGEROUS?

Pain, redness, heat, stiffness, or loss of mobility are common symptoms of this condition. If these symptoms persist, what was once an acute inflammation becomes chronic, lasting several years or even a lifetime. There are many types of inflammation and different reactions to them. However, abdominal inflammation, that terrible discomfort usually caused by the food we eat or how we live is undoubtedly one of the most common and most hated of all.

It occurs when the abdomen is more prominent than usual. Overeating rather than a severe illness, irritable bowel syndrome, or fluid retention are the leading causes. However, these are not the only factors that influence this phenomenon; there is a broader list of factors to be aware of.

Constipation: If you suffer from this dreaded condition, you will no doubt have noticed how often you tend to feel bloated; don't worry, this problem can be solved by eating a diet rich in fiber and fluids, as well as exercising.

Allergies: It is almost inevitable to have an allergy to something, and many of these cause inflammation of the abdomen; an example of this is lactose, and it is this allergy that tends to cause the accumulation of gas, so the best thing to do is to replace or avoid this food.

How fast you eat: Believe it or not, chewing your food too quickly is also bad for you, as your body may have excess air. Chewing slower will benefit you, but you will enjoy your food much more and feel fuller sooner.

Avoid processed foods: The excessive consumption of artificially sweetened foods will cause you to have extra air in your stomach, in addition to being high in sodium and low in fiber, so they will not be waiting to inflame you.

During pregnancy: Not only will this stage cause you to swell because of the baby, but because you are pregnant, the inflammation will continue, so constant monitoring for both you and the baby is essential.

DISEASES THAT CAN CAUSE IT

Various diseases can also cause this annoying symptom, and some of them are:

- Cardiovascular diseases
- Tumors
- Cirrhosis
- Appendicitis
- Gastric ulcer
- Diverticulitis
- Pancreatitis
- Premenstrual syndrome

WHY IS CHRONIC INFLAMMATION SO DANGEROUS, AND HOW CAN IT BE ELIMINATED?

Following are the signs of chronic inflammation

- Fatigue
- Various pains
- Dizziness
- Drowsiness
- Chronic pain
- Psychological complaints
- Gastrointestinal problems
- Provoking factors
- Constant stress
- Accumulation of toxins in the body
- Improper nutrition
- "leaky gut"
- Sedentary lifestyle and overweight
- Insufficient sleep
- Disturbed metabolism
- Genetic failure
- Inability to expel inflammation-promoting microorganisms

Many scientists worldwide have concluded that there is one phenomenon at the root of many chronic diseases. Cardiovascular and autoimmune diseases, neuro degenerative and mental disorders, cancer, and aging all have the same underlying cause. Chronic inflammation, which causes various health problems, was the key topic at the Congress of Nutritional Medicine in Holland in early September.

"Dr. Natalia Trofimova of Loodus Biospa says: "Chronic inflammation is such a serious cause of many diseases that absolutely everyone should think about what leads to it. It has specific indications, contributing factors, and opportunities for prevention and treatment."

Chronic inflammation is much more insidious than ordinary inflammation; it is often imperceptible at first and does not cause any immediately visible symptoms. We are clearer when the body is in normal acute inflammation, a protective response to invasion by harmful bacteria or viruses. Our body fights them off with the help of special cells, and when the job is done, the acute inflammation should go away, and the body's normal state should be restored.

In some cases, the inflammatory response persists, and the immune response continues, potentially damaging healthy cells and tissue. Chronic inflammation thus contributes to diseases from cardiovascular to autoimmune to cancer. It is also the main cause of aging.

How do you know if you are chronically inflamed? Because the symptoms are not as specific, this is more difficult than with ordinary inflammation. However, symptoms such as fatigue, various aches and pains, dizziness, drowsiness, chronic pain, sleep problems, psychological problems, and gastrointestinal problems are usually associated with chronic inflammation.

Several factors can trigger chronic inflammation. For example, constant stress, accumulation of toxins in the body (due to food intolerances, trans fats, pesticide residues), inappropriate diet (extra calories, sugar, lack of minerals), weakening of natural barriers ("leaky" intestines, skin, mucous membranes), sedentary lifestyle and excess weight, insufficient sleep, genetic failure and inability to remove microorganisms that cause inflammation from the body.

Fortunately, there are many ways to keep chronic inflammation under control or even eliminate it. In the case of food intolerance, you need to do a test and exclude everything the body cannot digest from the menu. You can also start using probiotics to improve bowel function. To reduce the amount of visceral fat, you should go through a program of therapeutic fasting, detox, or diet. Regular physical activity on an empty stomach also does not hurt—more rest, eliminating toxic substances and relationships, and a healthier lifestyle.

THE ROLE OF DIET

Some medicines can help reduce chronic inflammation. These include non-steroidal anti-inflammatory drugs, corticosteroids, metformin, and other anti-diabetic drugs. However, they should not be used alone if you suspect chronic inflammatory conditions.

Lifestyle changes play a central role in treating and preventing chronic inflammation. For example, exercise can help reduce blood levels of inflammatory biomarkers.

CHARACTERISTICS OF AN ANTI-INFLAMMATORY DIET

To reduce inflammation, you need to eat less inflammatory foods and focus on the foods that can help reduce the response. Avoid processed foods and base your diet on whole, nutrient-dense, antioxidant-rich foods. Antioxidants reduce free radicals in the body. These reactive molecules, or free radicals, are integral to metabolism. However, when there are too many of them, they can indicate inflammation.

The anti-inflammatory diet must include a healthy balance of protein, carbohydrates, and fatty acids in each meal of the day. In addition, you must ensure you are meeting your needs for vitamins, minerals, fiber, and water. Especially for people who are overweight or have metabolic syndrome, a low-carbohydrate diet can also reduce inflammation. Many people also rely on the Low Fodmap and find it a great help. In addition, a vegetarian diet has been shown to reduce inflammation, mainly due to its high levels of antioxidants and beneficial nutrients. Finally, a diet for fibromyalgia is often mentioned by patients who suffer from rheumatism and those who have chronic inflammatory reactions in the body.

The low glycemic index (a reduction in sugary drinks and refined carbohydrates in the diet). Low saturated and trans fats. It's necessary to eat less processed and fried foods and red meat.

An adequate intake of omega-3 fatty acids (fish, and nuts) has an anti-inflammatory effect.

Eat plenty of fruits and vegetables. They are a source of antioxidants and fiber, compounds with anti-inflammatory properties.

Presence of bioactive compounds: tea polyphenols, curcumin, minerals (zinc, selenium, magnesium), and vitamins (D, E).

The anti-inflammatory diet has been proven effective in many studies. The most important scientific review has shown that it can reduce the risk of at least 26 diseases associated with this phenomenon, including myocardial infarction, depression, pancreatic cancer, respiratory system cancer, and oral cavity cancer. Previously, an anti-inflammatory diet was associated with an 18% lower risk of death compared to people whose diet was the most different from it.

BREAKFAST RECIPES

BANANA OATMEAL MUFFINS

Breakfast muffins are convenient, easy, and a great way to use overripe bananas. In addition, they add sweetness to this recipe, so there is no added sugar.

Ingredients
- ½ cup of rolled oats
- 1 cup quick oats
- ½ tsp baking powder
- ½ tsp baking soda
- 3 bananas
- 2 eggs
- ¼ cup extra virgin olive oil

Cooking:
1. Set the oven temperature to 190 degrees and place the cupcake liners in a pan.
2. Mix oatmeal with baking powder and baking soda.
3. Add salt and thoroughly mix mashed bananas, eggs, and butter with the dry ingredients until a thick dough is formed.
4. Evenly distribute the batter among the prepared liners and put it in the oven for 20-25 minutes. Your dish is ready.

Nutrition Facts:
This recipe is a very good source of fiber and vitamin C.

Nutritional values per serving:
Calories 170 | Fats 9g (Trans 0) | Carbs 21g | Sugar 4 g|Sodium 121,5mg | Potassium 1021mg | Cholesterol 19,5mg

Active: 20-25 min ¬ **Total:** 40 min ¬ **Serving:** 6

BLUEBERRY CHIA PUDDING

This is an easy-to-make recipe; blueberry is rich in antioxidants that fight inflammation.

Ingredients:
- 1 cup almond milk
- ½ cup yogurt
- 6 tbsp chia seeds
- 2 tbsp maple syrup
- 1 cup blueberries

Cooking:
1. Add all ingredients to the container and refrigerate overnight!
2. In the morning, your mega tasty and healthy breakfast is ready
3. Add chia seeds first

Nutrition Facts:
This pudding is a good source of dietary fiber, calcium, antioxidants from the chia seeds and blueberries, and probiotics from the yogurt.

Nutritional values per serving:
Calories 226 | Fat 9g (Trans 0)| Carb: 33g | Sugars: 17g | Sodium 5,9mg | Potassium 278,5mg | Cholesterol 0g | Fiber11,8g

Active: 5 min ¬ **Total: Overnight** ¬ **Serving: 2**

OATMEAL WITH BERRIES

Adding chia seeds and berries adds more fiber and antioxidants to the meal. If yogurt and honey are added, the nutritional content will vary.

Ingredients:
- 1 banana
- 1 cup oatmeal
- 5floz (150ml) milk
- 3 tsp chia seeds
- 5,3oz (150g) of your favorite frozen berries
- honey
- yogurt (optional)

Cooking:
1. Lubricate the mold with oil, mash 1 banana, pour oatmeal over the banana, add milk and chia seeds and mix it all.
2. Top with your favorite frozen berries, and sprinkle with more coconut if desired.
3. When serving, you can add yogurt and honey
4. Bake for 25 minutes at 180°.

Nutrition Facts:

The recipe is a perfect source of fiber, protein, and essential vitamins and minerals, including vitamin C and calcium, reducing inflammation.

Nutritional values per serving:

Calories: 374 | Fat: 7g (Trans 0g) | Carbs: 65g | Sugars: 18g | Sodium 86,5mg | Potassium 638,6mg | Cholesterol 3,1mg

Active: 5 min ¬ **Total:** Overnight ¬ **Serving:**

OATMEAL COOKIES AND NUTS

The recipe is as simple as mixing, forming, and baking.

Ingredients:
- 2 eggs
- 5,3oz (150g) mashed pumpkin
- 0,09oz (2.5g) ground cinnamon
- 0,09oz (2,5g) vanilla
- 1 tsp of chia seeds
- 1 tsp flax seeds
- 1,7oz (48g) raw almonds
- 1,7oz (48g) raisins
- 6oz (170g) oatmeal

Cooking:
1. To begin, set the oven temperature to 180ºC and ready one or two trays.
2. Mix eggs with pumpkin, cinnamon, and vanilla in a bowl, and beat with a hand beater until everything is well integrated. Add the salt, rolled oats, chia and flax seeds, and almonds.
3. Combine well to have a homogeneous dough and form cookies taking small portions with a few teaspoons.
4. Bake for about 15-18 minutes or until golden to taste.

Nutrition Facts:

While comparably low in calories and sugar to other cookies, it includes some minerals and vitamins like calcium and iron.

Nutritional values per serving:

Calories 184 | Fat 8.2g (Trans 0g) | Carbs 16.7g | Sugars: 7.4g | Fiber 6,8g | Sodium 1,9mg | Potassium 386,3mg | Cholesterol 0 mg

Active: 15 min ¬ **Total:** 30 min ¬ **Serving:** 5

PUMPKIN AND OATMEAL PANCAKES

I recommend you roast or cook a huge pumpkin and have reserves of its minced meat in the fridge or freezer because it can give a lot of play.

Ingredients:
- 3oz (85g) cooked pumpkin
- 2 eggs
- 1 tsp sodium bicarbonate
- ground cinnamon to taste
- vanilla essence to taste
- 4oz (113g) oatmeal

Cooking:
1. To quickly prepare the pumpkin, we can steam it in the microwave. Put in a container suitable for the microwave and cook -with steam function, if we have it- until it is very tender about 10 minutes.
2. Mix eggs in a bowl. Add the pumpkin, baking soda, flour, and spices and beat the mixture until it is even.
3. Grease a griddle or nonstick skillet and heat it on medium power. Slowly pour portions of the batter onto the skillet, shaping them into a round form.
4. Depending on the size, we will get about 4-6 units. We can brown them to taste.

Nutrition Facts:
This recipe provides a variety of vitamins and minerals, including vitamin A and manganese, which plays a role in bone health and metabolism.

Nutritional values per serving:
Calories: 75 kcal | Fat 1 g (Trans 0g) | Carbs 11 g | Sugars: 2 g | Fiber 10,2g | Sodium 38,8 mg | Potassium 764,3 mg | Cholesterol 2,4mg

Active: 15 min¬ **Total:** 20 min¬ **Serving:** 4

OATMEAL AND APPLE COOKIES

These cookies are tender in texture because they do not contain butter, eggs, or oil.

Ingredients:
- 9oz (255g) apple puree
- 3oz (85g) fine rolled oats
- 2-3oz (50-80g) sliced raw almonds
- 1 teaspoon ground almonds
- 1 pinch of low sodium salt

Cooking:
1. Preheating your oven to 180°C and greasing a baking tray.
2. Combine the apple sauce, oat flakes, salt, and cinnamon in a bowl, thoroughly mixing until a smooth consistency is achieved. Optionally, add other ingredients, such as almonds, to suit your taste.
3. Create circular cookies by shaping the dough and arranging them on the baking tray.
4. Once you've placed the cookies in the oven, bake them for 10-13 minutes until fully cooked, and your delicious dessert will be ready for consumption.

Nutrition Facts:
These cookies are a low-fat and low-calorie option. In addition, they contain some healthy fiber from oats and almonds.

Nutritional values per serving:
Calories 50 | Fat 1.5g (Trans 0g) | Carbs 9g | Sugars 3.5g| Sodium 165,5 mg | Potassium 362,8mg | Cholesterol 0mg | Fiber 11,1g

Active: 15 min ¬ **Total:** 30 min ¬ **Serving:** 5-6

OMELET WITH EGGPLANT

The use of extra virgin olive oil provides healthy monounsaturated fats. Overall, this is a healthy and delicious dish to enjoy for breakfast.

Ingredients:
- 1 small striped eggplan
- 1 small or medium chive
- 1 tbsp ground turmeric
- 1 tbsp ground cumin
- 3floz (100ml) vegetable broth
- 5 egg whites
- 1 tsp mustard
- 1 tbsp milk (optional: 1 tbsp yeast)
- fresh parsley per taste
- black pepper per taste
- 2 tsp extra virgin olive oil
- low sodium salt per taste

Cooking:
1. Wash the eggplant. Cut into small cubes of more or less the same size. Finely chop the onion.
2. Add spring onion in warm olive oil with salt and cook over low heat for 5 minutes. Follow the eggplant, season it with spices, and mix all the ingredients well.
3. Cook for 10-15 minutes, occasionally stirring, until very tender.
4. Beat the egg whites with the mustard, milk, yeast, and a pinch of pepper and salt. Pour over the pan, and cook over low heat for about 8-10 minutes.
5. Serve with washed and chopped parsley.

Nutrition Facts:
Egg whites are rich source of protein, while eggplant is high in fiber, vitamin C, and potassium.

Nutritional values per serving:
Calories 129 cal | Fa 4g (Trans 0g)| Carbs: 9g | Sugar 5g | Fiber 5,7g | Sodium 229,3mg | Potassium 185,5 mg | Cholesterol 254,4mg

Active: 25 min ¬ **Total:** 30 min ¬ **Serving:** 1

COCONUT AND HEMP BARS

It's a great inflammation-fighting breakfast on-the-go, not to mention a good source of protein.

Ingredients:
- 1 cup of organic hemp hearts
- 1 cup of shredded organic coconut
- 1 cup of almond butter
- 1/3 cup organic maple syrup
- 1 teaspoon of ground cinnamon

Cooking:
1. Preheat the oven to 160 degrees Celsius (320°F)
2. Spread the coconut on a baking sheet for 5-10 minutes or until completely golden. At the same time, mix the hemp hearts, almond butter, maple syrup, and ground cinnamon in a bowl.
3. Add the toasted coconut and mix well. Press the mixture into a previously buttered baking pan and freeze for at least three hours.
4. Subsequently, cut into squares of the size of your preference. Ideally, you will get 15 servings with these proportions

Nutrition Facts:
This recipe is a good source of protein and dietary fiber. Hemp hearts are an excellent source of plant-based protein and contain omega-3 and omega-6 fatty acids.

Nutritional values per serving:
Calories 262 | Fat 21g (Trans 0g) | Carbs12g | Sugars 5g | Fiber 9,8g | Sodium 68,4mg | Potassium 694,3mg | Cholesterol 3mg

Active: 5 min ¬ **Total:** 10 min¬ **Serving:** 1

CHIA PUDDING WITH COCONUT AND TURMERIC

This chia seed pudding with turmeric and red berries contains anti-inflammatory nutrients that strengthen our immune system and keep our defenses at their best.

Ingredients:
- 4 tablespoons chia seeds
- ½ teaspoon turmeric
- 1 teaspoon honey
- 4 ½oz (125g) coconut yogurt (no sugar)
- 7floz (200ml) coconut drink
- 1 handful of red berries
- 1 handful blueberries

Cooking:
1. The night before, mix the chia seeds, turmeric, yogurt, honey, and coconut drink in a bowl and stir so that everything is well combined.
2. Put in the fridge and let rest overnight.
3. In the morning, serve with some red fruits and blueberries.

Nutrition Facts:
This chia pudding with coconut and turmeric is a source of fiber, healthy fats, and antioxidants. Chia is rich in omega-3s, which are beneficial for heart health and can help reduce inflammation.

Nutritional values per serving:
Calories 237 cal | Fat 12g (Trans 0g) | Carbs 26g | Sugar 9g | Fiber 16,9g | Sodium 156,9mg | Potassium 574,6mg | Cholesterol 0mg

Active: 5 min ¬ **Total:** 10 min ¬ **Serving:** 1

PORRIDGE WITH GOLDEN MILK

It is an ideal breakfast for winter because it is satiating, warm and the turmeric, cinnamon, and ginger are spices that, in addition to giving a super tasty flavor, are anti-inflammatory,

Ingredients:
- 2,8oz (80g) oat flakes
- ½ tablespoon almond cream
- 1 glass of coconut drink
- ¼ teaspoon turmeric
- ¼ teaspoon cinnamon
- pinch nutmeg
- ½ teaspoon honey
- blueberries
- desiccated coconut

Cooking:
1. Heat the water in a small saucepan and add oats and almond cream when it boils. Stir until the cream dissolves.
2. Add the coconut drink, turmeric, cinnamon, ginger, nutmeg, and honey, and stir for another couple of minutes until the porridge has a creamy texture.
3. We transfer to a breakfast bowl and serve with the most toppings we like.

Nutrition Facts:
The spices in this recipe have anti-inflammatory properties. In addition, the desiccated coconut provides a source of healthy fats and fiber.

Nutritional values per serving:
Calories 381 cal | Fat 14.8g | Carbs 54.6g (Trans 0)| Sugars 14.6g

Active: 5 min ¬ **Total:** 10 min¬ **Serving:** 1

FLUFFY ARTICHOKE FRITTATA

It's a very quick and easy recipe, and we can vary the filling with seasonal vegetables.

Ingredients:
- 8-10 artichoke hearts
- 2-3 eggs
- 4 whites,
- 4,2floz (125 ml) of milk
- light cream 1 tbsp
- ½ teaspoon of turmeric
- 1 teaspoon of brewer's or nutritional yeast (optional)
- Provencal herbs to taste
- black pepper
- low sodium salt
- extra virgin olive oil
- grated cheese to taste (optional)

Cooking:
1. Start by cooking the artichokes in water until they become tender but firm.
2. Preheat your oven to 350°F(180ºC) and butter a pan, dish, or skillet suitable for baking with olive oil. Divide the egg yolks and whites into separate bowls. Beat the egg yolks with milk or cream, turmeric, yeast, and herbs, then season the mixture with salt and pepper.
3. Whisk the egg whites until they are almost stiff, then combine both mixtures. Fill the bread with the mixture and spread the artichokes over it. Finally, sprinkle some pepper and add cheese if desired. Bake for approximately 25-30 minutes.

Nutrition Facts:
This recipe contains foods that are a good source of fiber, vitamin C, antioxidants, protein, vitamins, minerals, calcium, vitamin D, and healthy fats.

Nutritional values per serving:
Calories 155 | Carbs 10g | Fat 8g (Trans 0g) | Sugar 3g | Sodium 247,5mg | Potassium 271,4 | Cholesterol 103,4mg | Fiber 2g

Active: 35 min ¬ **Total:** 40 min ¬ **Serving:** 2-3

GRANOLA BOWL

The recipe is high in carbohydrates, with a significant amount of dietary fiber and sugars, making it a good option for breakfast to keep you satiated throughout the morning.

Ingredients:
- frozen berries
- 3½floz (100ml) coconut water
- 2 tbsp acai powder
- 1oz (28g) granola
- 1 frozen banana
- fruit to decorate (in this case, we have chosen mango and blueberries).

Cooking:
1. The first thing is added in the specific blender to make smoothies (see on Amazon) a frozen banana, a cup of frozen berries, half a glass of coconut water, and a tablespoon of açai powder.
2. Mix everything in the blender until it becomes a thick liquid. Next, once everything we have said is blended, it is reversed in a container, be it a bowl or a cup for breakfast. Finally, we will decorate the bowl as we like by adding granola, mango, and blueberry cereals.

Nutrition Facts:
The recipe's ingredients contain vitamin C, vitamin K, and potassium.

Nutritional values per serving:
Calories 536 | Fat 12g (Trans 0g) | Carbs 98g | Sugars 43g | Fiber 14,7g | Sodium 269,4mg | Potassium 160,4mg | Cholesterol 0,5mg

Active: 5 min ¬ **Total:** 10 min ¬ **Serving:** 1

ACAI BOWL WITH CHOCOLATE

This acai dish is ideal when you need much energy to play sports or start the day off right. It is very easy and fast to do.

Ingredients:
- 2oz (56g) semi-frozen fruit
- 2oz (56g) fresh fruit
- 2 tbsp acai powder
- 1oz (28g) greek yogurt
- 1 tbsp almond cream
- chocolate chips optional
- 2 tbsp pumpkin seeds

Cooking:
1. Put the frozen fruits, the acai powder, 4 tablespoons of yogurt (Greek is preferable), and fresh fruit (blueberries and raspberries) in the Moulinex blender (see Amazon). Finally, vegetable milk is added. Mix everything in the blender for a few minutes. Once blended, put it in a bowl to start decorating the plate.
2. For decoration, it is recommended to put a few tablespoons of Greek yogurt in circles on top, diluted with a bit of milk so that its texture is less thick.

Nutrition Facts:
The Acai bowl is a good source of Vitamin C, potassium, and calcium.

Nutritional values per serving:
Calorie 240 | Fat 11g (Trans 0) | Carbs 28g | Sugars 16g | Fiber 24,9g | Sodium 115mg | Potassium 1170 mg | Cholesterol 0g

Active: 25 min ¬ **Total:** 30 min ¬ **Serving:** 1

MINI PEAR CRUMBLE WITH WALNUTS

The sugar-free recipe is high in fiber, perfect for satisfying you until lunchtime.

Ingredients:
- 2 pears
- 2 pinches cinnamon
- ½ teaspoon coconut oil (melted)
- 1,7oz (50g) thick oat flakes
- 1 handful walnuts
- 1 teaspoon honey

Cooking:
1. Start to preheat the oven to 390°F(200°C)
2. Peel and chop the pears into small pieces and divide them between two small containers.
3. Add the cinnamon and coconut oil and mix well. Bake for 20 minutes until the pear is tender.
4. While the pear is baking, combine the rolled oats, chopped walnuts, and honey in a bowl.
5. When the pear is ready, take it out of the oven and cover the surface with the oats,
6. Bake for 15 more minutes until the oats are toasted.

Nutrition Facts:
The recipe contains healthy fats from walnuts and coconut oil, complex carbohydrates from the oat flakes, and natural sweetness from the pears and honey.

Nutritional values per serving:
Calories 243 kcal | Fat 9g (Trans 0g) | Carbs 32g | Sugars 12 g | Fiber 8,2g | Sodium 2,1mg | Potassium 395,1 mg | Cholesterol 0g

Active: 45 min ¬ **Total:** 60 min ¬ **Serving:** 2

OATMEAL AND COCOA PORRIDGE

It is a perfect breakfast to warm up in the morning, keeping you sat until lunchtime.

Ingredients:
- 2½oz (71g) oats
- 6floz (180ml) water
- 6floz (180ml) non-dairy milk
- 1 tablespoon almond cream
- ½ tablespoon honey
- 1 tablespoon pure cocoa
- 1 tablespoon flaxseeds (optional)
- 1 handful blueberries

Cooking:
1. Soak the flax seeds the night before.
2. In a small pan, bring the water to a boil. Add the oats and stir. When the water is absorbed, add the vegetable milk. Continue stirring while adding the almond cream, honey, and cocoa, and keep on the heat until a creamy texture is obtained.
3. Remove from the heat, serve in a bowl, and add the fruit on top.

Nutrition Facts:

The cocoa provides a delicious chocolate flavor while also offering antioxidants. Blueberries are a rich source of vitamins, minerals, and antioxidants.

Active: 5 min ¬ Total: Overnight ¬ Serving: 1

Nutritional values per serving:

Calories 327 | Fat 10g | Carbs 53g |Sugars 13g | Fiber 6,8g | Sodium 3,2mg | Potassium 257,6mg | Cholesterol 0mg

MAIN DISH RECIPES

WARM SALAD WITH PINE NUTS, TOMATO, AND BASIL

It is a perfect breakfast to warm up in the morning, keeping you sat until lunchtime.

Ingredients:
- 1lb (455g) mix of tender sprouts
- 8 pear tomatoes
- 1 clove garlic
- 4 sprigs of basil
- 2 tablespoons balsamic vinegar
- 1 red onion
- ¾oz (20g) of peeled pine nuts
- extra virgin olive oil
- pepper

Cooking:
1. Begin by preheating your oven to 60°F(140ºC). After washing and drying the basil and peeling the garlic, crush them with 1 dl of oil.
2. Cut the tomatoes in half lengthwise, wash and dry them, and arrange them on a baking sheet. Brush them with the basil oil, sprinkle with a few drops of vinegar, and add the pine nuts before baking them for about an hour.
3. Cut the onion after peeling it and clean the salad sprouts.
4. Dress them with the remaining vinegar, oil, and salt, ensuring they are well coated on all sides. Mix in the pine nuts and onion.
5. Place four pastry rings on separate plates and fill them with the prepared mixture. Carefully place the tomatoes on top, remove the rings, and serve the salad immediately.

Nutrition Facts:

This salad is a great source of fiber, healthy fats, vitamin C, vitamin A, potassium, vitamin K, and manganese.

Nutritional values per serving:

Calories 260 | Fat 20g | Carbs 16g | Sugars 7g | Fiber 11,9g | Sodium 143,5mg | Potassium 1586,5mg | Cholesterol 0g

Active: 30 min ¬ **Total:** 90 min ¬ **Serving:** 4

CASSEROLE WITH CABBAGE

This recipe is low in calories and carbohydrates and provides a good dietary fiber and protein source.

Ingredients:
- 1lb (455g) of cabbage
- 1 tbsp olive oil
- 3,3floz (100ml) of water
- low sodium salt
- pepper
- 3,5oz (100g) vegan mozzarella
- 2 tbsp vegan sour cream
- nutmeg

Cooking:
1. Cut the cabbage into fine strips after washing it.
2. Briefly saute the cabbage in a large saucepan with heated oil. Pour in water.
3. Cover and cook the cabbage for 12 minutes. Add salt and pepper.
4. Cut the mozzarella into small cubes while it cooks.
5. Mix sour cream into the cabbage, and season it with nutmeg.
6. Sprinkle the casserole with the cheese.
7. Let the casserole bake at 200 degrees for about 15 minutes.

Nutrition Facts:
It is enriched with vitamin C, vitamin K, and calcium.

Nutritional values per serving:
Calories 130 | Fat: 9g (Trans 0)| Carbs 7g | Sugars 3g | Fiber 4g | Sodium 181,3mg | Potassium 729mg | Cholesterol 0 g

Active: 10 min ¬ **Total:** 30 min ¬ **Serving:** 2

MUSHROOM PAN WITH SPINACH

Enjoy this recipe loaded with comfort foods to fight inflammation

Ingredients:
- 17,6oz (500g) mixed mushrooms
- 2 garlic cloves
- 20 sage leaves
- 9oz (260g) spinach
- low sodium salt and pepper
- 1 tsp zest of lemon

Cooking:
1. Clean and chop the mushrooms. Cut the Garlic into fine slices. Fry the mushrooms on both sides in a pan with olive oil. When they have some color, push the mushrooms aside and put olive oil in the middle of the pan.
2. Fry the sage leaves and Garlic in it. The sage leaves should be slightly crispy.
3. Then mix the mushrooms, sage, and Garlic, add the spinach, and let them wilt for 1-2 minutes. Season with salt, pepper, and lemon zest.

Nutrition Facts:
It is enriched with vitamins and minerals, especially vitamin C, iron, and potassium.

Nutritional values per serving:
Calories 205 kcal | Fat 10.3g | Carbs 20.6g | Sugars 3.8g | Fiber 5g | Sodium 506mg | Potassium 976,5mg Cholesterol 0g

Active: 5 min ¬ **Total:** 10 min ¬ **Serving:** 4

MUSHROOM AND ZUCCHINI SPAGHETTI

Packed with flavor and nutrition, this recipe is vegan and gluten-free.

Ingredients:
- 1lb (455g) mushrooms
- 2 zucchini
- 1 red onion
- 1 clove garlic
- a handful of cashews
- 6-7 chive stalks
- 4 tablespoons of olive oil
- pepper and sea salt
- 9oz (250g) firm tofu
- 1 tablespoon tamari
- ½ teaspoon smoked paprika
- 1 tablespoon nutritional yeast
- 1 tablespoon turmeric

Cooking:
1. Take the tofu out of the package, wrap it in a cloth or kitchen paper, put a weight (for example, a cutting board) on top, and let it dry well.
2. Meanwhile, wash the zucchini, remove them, and cut them into spirals with a spiralizer or thin, long strips with the help of a mandolin or peeler.
3. Cook the zucchini spirals in boiling salted water for 2 minutes, then cool them in a bowl of cold water. Drain and set aside.
4. Slice and fry the onion in a pan with 2 tablespoons of olive oil for 8-10 minutes over low heat. Add the zucchini spirals, salt, and pepper, and sauté briefly. Sprinkle with half of the chopped chives.

Nutrition Facts:

This dish contains protein, fiber, vitamins C and K, potassium and manganese, B vitamins, copper, selenium, and potassium.

Nutritional values per serving:

Calories 370 | Fat 28g | Carbs16g | Sugars 6g | Fiber 8,1g | Sodium 24,1mg | 907,6mg | Cholesterol 0mg

Active: 10 min ¬ **Total:** 30 min ¬ **Serving:** 4

BUCKWHEAT TIMBALE, PEAS, AND TOMATO WITH SPROUTS

This dish is a good source of dietary fiber and protein.

Ingredients:
- 1lb (455g) buckwheat
- 7 floz (800 ml) of water
- 2 large carrots
- 1 large, very ripe tomato
- 7oz (200g) peas
- ½oz (15g) radish sprouts
- turmeric
- oregano
- peppers
- extra virgin olive oil

Cooking:
1. Cook the buckwheat and let it cool.
2. Peel a carrot and cut it into small dice. Put a pan on the fire with a little olive oil and cook the carrot with the pan covered. After about 15 minutes, or when it is tender, remove and reserve. Repeat the process with the chopped tomato.
3. Cook the peas in salted water for 7 minutes. Reserve 100 g of peas to decorate, sauteed in a pan with a little olive oil, and seasoned.
4. Divide the buckwheat into three equal parts. Crush one part with the tomato, another with the carrot, and the last with 100 g peas. Add to all a jet of oil and salt and pepper.
5. Season as follows: carrot puree with turmeric, tomato with paprika, and peas with oregano. Integrate the spices well and reserve.
6. With the help of a stainless steel ring, on a plate, arrange the first layer of the pea mixture, the second of the carrot, and the third of the tomato. Remove the hoop. Decorate with the reserved sauteed peas and sprouts.

Nutrition Facts:
This dish is a good source of healthy fats, vitamins, and minerals, while buckwheat is a good source of complex carbohydrates.

Nutritional values per serving:
Calories 378 | Fat 7g (Trans 0)| Carbs 67g | Sugars 8g | Fiber 12,2g | Sodium ,4mg | Potassium 210mg | Cholesterol 0g

Active: 20 min ¬ **Total:** 30 min ¬ **Serving:** 4

TORTELLINI BROCCOLI CASSEROLE

A delicious family meal

Ingredients:
- half a white onion
- 1 small clove of garlic
- 1 head broccoli
- 1½lb (225g) of tomato passata
- 6,7floz (192ml) of water
- 17,6oz (500g) tortellini
- 1 tsp oregano
- 1 tsp thyme
- 1 teaspoon basil
- 1½oz (45g) Parmesan

Cooking:
1. Cook the broccoli in water for 5 minutes after washing and breaking them off.
2. Finely chop the onion and garlic after peeling them.
3. Preheat the oven to 90°F or 180 degrees for top and bottom heat.
4. Sauté the broccoli, onion, and garlic in a little olive oil.
5. Pour tomato passata and water into the pan, and let it boil for about 10 minutes.
6. Garnish with oregano, thyme, and basil.
7. Place the tortellini in a casserole dish, and cover it with the sauce.
8. Sprinkle Parmesan on top.
9. Bake the casserole until golden brown for around 25 minutes.

Nutrition Facts:

This recipe contains vitamin C, K, A, calcium, and iron.

Nutritional values per serving:

Calories 376 | Fat 9.9g (Trans 0g)| Carbs 56g |Sugars 10g | Fiber 5,7g | Sodium 560,9mg | Potassium 316,8mg | Cholesterol 36,4mg

Active: 35 min ¬ **Total:** 50 min ¬ **Serving:** 4

CASSEROLE WITH KOHLRABI

Nutritionally, this recipe provides a good source of dietary fiber and protein while being moderate in calories and fat.

Ingredients:
- 10floz (295ml) vegetable broth
- 1lb (454) g kohlrabi
- low sodium salt
- 10½oz (298g) wholemeal penne
- 2 small onions
- 1 zucchini
- 2 tbsp olive oil
- 1 tbsp flour
- 10floz (295ml) plant milk
- 5oz (142g) of peas
- 1 bunch of parsley
- nutmeg
- pepper
- 1½oz (40g) cheese

Cooking:
1. Add vegetable broth to a pan and boil it. Wash the kohlrabi, peel it, and cut it into small cubes.
2. Let the kohlrabi simmer in the vegetable broth for about 15 minutes.
3. Cook noodles in boiling water.
4. Meanwhile, peel and finely chop the onions. Sautee the onions until translucent in olive oil.
5. Wash the courgettes thoroughly and cut them into thin slices. Dust with flour and sweat, stirring constantly.
6. Once the kohlrabi is cooked, strain it and keep the vegetable broth aside.
7. Combine the vegetable broth and milk with the roux, and whisk everything together. Let the whole thing come to a boil. Add the zucchini and peas and let the sauce simmer for about ten minutes.
8. Add the parsley to the sauce and season with nutmeg, salt, and pepper.
9. Drain the noodles and put them in a casserole dish.
10. Spread the kohlrabi, the vegetable sauce, and the cheese on the pasta one after the other.
11. Bake the casserole at 200 degrees for about 25 to 30 minutes.

Nutrition Facts:

This recipe is a good source of fiber, protein, vitamins A, C, K, and B-complex, calcium, iron, magnesium, and potassium.

Nutritional values per serving:

Calories 354 kcal | Fat 11g(Trans 0,1g) | Carbs 49 g | Sugars 9 g | Fiber 1,3g | Sodium 30,1mg | Potassium 127,4 mg | Cholesterol 23,6mg

Active: 30 min ¬ **Total:** 60 min ¬ **Serving:** 4

CHILI CON TOFU

This recipe is high in dietary fiber and protein, making it a filling and satisfying meal.

Ingredients:
- 2 onions
- 4 tbsp olive oil for frying
- 2 small chili peppers
- 3 tsp cumin
- 2 tsp paprika powder
- 1½lb (680g) tomatoes, sieved or chunky
- 2 tbsp paprika
- 9oz (255g) tofu, natural or smoked
- 9oz kidney beans (255g)
- 10oz (285g) corn
- 2 tsp cocoa powder
- 1 pinch
- cinnamon

Cooking:
1. Peel the onions and cut them. Heat some oil in a saucepan and fry the onions until translucent.
2. Chop the chilies and add them to the pot, along with some cumin and paprika powder. After 5 minutes, add tomatoes and cook.
3. Add the vegetable broth to the pot and let it simmer over medium heat for approximately 30 minutes.
4. While the broth is cooking, chop the peppers into small pieces.
5. Dice or crumble the tofu to get it close to its original consistency. Cook tofu in hot oil in a pan.
6. Add the peppers, fried tofu, beans, and corn to the chili con tofu after 30 minutes of cooking. Let everything cook for another 30 minutes.
7. Finally, add cocoa and cinnamon to the chili con tofu and season to taste.

Nutrition Facts:
It contains vitamins and minerals such as C, A, iron, and potassium.

Nutritional values per serving:
Calories 246 | Fat 11g | Carbs 28g |Sugars: 8g | Fiber 8,3g | Sodium 307,7mg | Potassium 614,5mg | Cholesterol 0

Active: 15 min ¬ **Total:** 60 min ¬ **Serving:** 4

CAULIFLOWER POTATO CURRY

This recipe is a good source of dietary fiber.

Ingredients:
- 1 small cauliflower
- 5-6 potatoes
- 2 handfuls kale leaves, stemless, roughly chopped
- 1 small piece of fresh ginger
- 2 onions
- 2 tsp turmeric powder
- 1 tsp paprika powder
- 1 tbsp curry powder
- 1 small red chili
- ½ tsp mustard seeds
- ½ lemon
- ½ bunch of fresh coriander
- 1 tbsp tomato paste
- 5-6 small tomatoes
- 1 tbsp coconut oil
- 17floz (502 ml) vegetable broth
- 1 tbsp apricot puree

Cooking:
1. To start, cleanse and trim the cauliflower and kale. Then, peel the potatoes, halve them, and finely chop the ginger. Cut the chili pepper lengthwise and dice it into small pieces. Finally, coarsely chop the peeled onions.
2. Heat coconut oil in a saucepan and briefly sauté onions, ginger, and chili. Then briefly add the turmeric, paprika, curry, mustard seeds, tomato paste, and saute. Deglaze everything with vegetable broth and cook the potatoes and cauliflower florets for 10 minutes over medium heat.
3. After washing and cleaning the tomatoes, cut them into pieces and add them to the stew. Squeeze the lemon juice and add it, along with the apricot puree. Let everything simmer for another 10 to 15 minutes. Just before the end of cooking, add the prepared kale. This should only steam briefly and not overcook. Finally, season the curry with salt, pepper, lemon juice, and chopped coriander.

Nutrition Facts:
This recipe contains vitamins C, K, B6, potassium, and iron.

Nutritional values per serving:
Calories 221 | Fat 4g (Trans 0,1g) | Carbs 44g | Sugars 9g | Fiber 22,9g | Sodium 345,2 mg | Potassium 2502,2 | Cholesterol 0g

Active: 15 min ¬ **Total:** 20 min ¬ **Serving:** 4

POKE BOWL

Fats are essential for our survival. This easy recipe is simple, incredibly delicious, and provides healthy fats.

Ingredients:
- 3½oz (103g) of brown rice
- 2oz (57g) of tempeh
- 2oz (57g) of salmon
- ¼ avocado
- 1oz (28g) of edamame
- 1,7oz (50g) of lettuce
- 1,7oz (50g) cherry tomatoes
- coconut oil
- soy sauce
- sesame

Cooking:
1. Cook in accordance with package directions. We recommend fragrant jasmine rice.
2. Meanwhile, you can cut the tempeh into strips and fry it in a pan with coconut oil.
3. Wash the lettuce and put it in a bowl.
4. The warm rice is now on top.
5. Halve the tomatoes and arrange them next to the rice.
6. Also, add the edamame and tempeh alongside the rice for a colorful bowl later.
7. The salmon stays raw, is cut into cubes, and can now be added to the bowl.
8. The ripe avocado is carefully sliced, closing the circle around the rice.
9. Now pour a few dashes of soy sauce over your bowl and sprinkle sesame seeds.
10. Real Poké Bowl pros now have fresh coriander up their sleeves.

Nutrition Facts:

It is enriched with vitamins, minerals, and healthy fats such as; A, C, D, K, and E, Omega-6

Nutritional values per serving:

Calories 540 | Fat 25g (Trans 0g)| Carbs 49g | Sugars 4g | Fiber 5,8g | Sodium 141,7mg | Potassium 418,8 | Cholesterol 31,2mg

Active: 5 min ¬ **Total:** 10 min ¬ **Serving:** 1

VEGETABLE CAKES

Comfort food for your gut.

Ingredients:
- 2 eggs
- 10½oz (297g) Vegetables (e.g., zucchini, carrots, leeks, onions)
- 1 teaspoon parsley, chopped
- 2oz (57g) Flour
- 1oz (28g) Oatmeal
- 3½oz (99g) Cheese.
- curry powder
- pepper
- paprika powder
- 1 tbsp extra virgin olive oil

Cooking:
1. Chop or grate the vegetables very finely, and grate the cheese. Stir in the eggs, rolled oats, and flour, and season well.
2. Heat the oil in a pan, add small cakes with a tablespoon, and fry them carefully.

Nutrition Facts:

This recipe provides a good source of protein, dietary fiber, and essential vitamins and minerals from the vegetables.

Nutritional values per serving:

Calories 264 kcal | Sugars 3.3 g | Fat 14.11g (Trans 0g | Carbs 20.21g | Fiber 1,3g | Sodium 43mg | Potassium 168,4mg | Cholesterol 26,5mg

Active: 25 min¬ **Total:** 40 min¬ **Serving:** 4

ZUCCHINI-SPAGHETTI

The addition of cream cheese adds a creamy texture to the dish

Ingredients:
- 1 zucchini
- 1 tbsp olive oil
- 2 tomatoes
- 2 tbsp mineral water
- 3 tbsp tomato paste
- 1 tsp heaped cream cheese
- low sodium salt and pepper
- herbs

Cooking:
1. Peel the zucchini into strips with a paring knife - like spaghetti or tagliatelle.
2. Fry the zucchini in a little olive oil. Meanwhile, chop the tomatoes and add them. Then add the mineral water (this will help the zucchini soften and wrap around the fork better). Add tomato paste and any amount of cream cheese (I recommend: 2 tsp). Salt, pepper, and add the herbs. Season if necessary (e.g., with paprika powder or gyros spice). Simmer a little more.

Nutrition Facts:
This recipe is a great source of fiber, potassium, vitamin C, vitamin A, and antioxidants.

Nutritional values per serving:
Calories 165 cal | Carbs 12g | Fat 12g | Sugar 8.76g | Fiber 6,7g | Sodium 394,6mg | Potassium 737mg | Cholesterol 0mg

Active: 15 min ¬ **Total:** 30 min ¬ **Serving:** 4

ZUCCHINI LASAGNA

The dish is versatile, and you can add or replace ingredients to suit your preferences

Ingredients:
- 2,2lb (998g) zucchini, big fat
- 1 large onion
- 1 garlic clove
- 1,1oz (31,2g) ground beef
- 1 tbsp tomato paste
- 1 can tomatoes, chunky
- 1 pack cream cheese (7oz/198g)
- 3,3floz (97,6ml) milk
- sour cream (optional)
- 5,2oz (147g) cheese, grated
- olive oil
- low sodium salt and pepper
- paprika powder, noble sweet
- oregano
- thyme
- parsley chopped

Cooking:
1. Wash zucchini and cut lengthways into finger-thick slices. Fry on both sides in olive oil in a pan, then drain on kitchen paper. Alternatively, brush the slices with olive oil, add a little salt, and brown them on the top rack with the grill function in the oven. However, that takes longer.
2. To start, chop the onion into small pieces and sautee it in a pan with a small amount of olive oil until it becomes translucent. Then, add the pressed garlic cloves and sautee for a short period. After that, add the minced meat to the pan and fry it until it crumbles.
3. When the meat has turned color, season with salt, pepper, and paprika powder, add 1 tablespoon of tomato paste, stir in, and sweat for a minute.
4. Add the tomatoes and season with oregano, thyme, salt, pepper, and paprika. Simmer for 10 minutes on a low flame, and add the chopped parsley at the end.
5. Combine the milk with the cream cheese, then mix in the sour cream. Add salt, pepper, and a small amount of nutmeg, and incorporate around 50 grams of spreadable cheese.
6. Line a lasagna dish or other casserole dish with zucchini slices. Spread a few spoonfuls of minced tomato sauce on top, a layer of cream cheese sauce on top, and zucchini slices on top. Keep layering until all the ingredients are used up. The top layer should be tomato mince sauce. Sprinkle them with the remaining cheese.
7. Bake the zucchini lasagne in a preheated oven at 200 °C top/bottom heat for approx. 30 minutes until golden brown.
8. A small fresh salad goes well with it.

Nutrition Facts:
The recipe contains significant amounts of vitamins A, C, and K, calcium, phosphorus, and zinc.

Nutritional values per serving:
Calories 504 | Fat 17.2g (Trans 0,1g) | Carbs 14.9g | Fiber 4,3g | Sugars 8.2g | Sodium 353,2mg | Potassium 1209mg | Cholesterol 163,2mg

Active: 25 min ¬ Total: 40 min ¬ Serving: 4

VEGETARIAN MEATBALLS

The recipe can be made ahead of time and reheated, making it a convenient option for meal prep.

Ingredients:
- 34floz(1l) vegetable broth
- 5,2oz (147g) rice
- 5,2oz (147g) Emmental
- 2 carrots
- 2 large onion
- 2 egg
- low sodium salt and pepper
- 3 tbsp herbs, mixed, frozen
- breadcrumbs
- clarified butter

Cooking:
1. Bring the broth to a boil, add the rice, and cook for 15 minutes. It should still be a little "al dente." Drain the rice and let cool.
2. Tip: You can also use leftovers from the previous day.
3. The rice should be pretty flavorful.
4. Grate the cheese, clean and grate the carrots (whether you grate the cheese and carrots finely or coarsely is up to your taste). Finely dice the onions.
5. Mix the rice, cheese, carrots, onions, and eggs. Stir in pepper (plenty), salt, and herbs. Now stir in the breadcrumbs until the mixture has some consistency. Then let it swell for about 15 minutes. Check whether the mass can be formed into a patty under pressure in the hands. If so, then roll them lightly in breadcrumbs.
6. Fry in plenty of clarified butter over low heat until golden brown on both sides. After frying on kitchen paper, drain off the fat.

Nutrition Facts:
The recipe provides fiber, essential micronutrients, vitamins A and C, and calcium.

Nutritional values per serving:
Calories 531 kcal | Fat 28g (Trans 0g) | Carbs 49g | Sugar 5g | Fiber 3,5g | Sodium 127mg | Potassium 199,4mg | Cholesterol 2,2mg

Active: 45 min ¬ Total: 80 min ¬ Serving: 4

SAUSAGE GOULASH AND MINCED MEAT

Reduce inflammation and improve digestion due to its capsaicin content.

Ingredients:
- 1,7oz (48,2g) bacon, fatter, finely diced
- 4 Sausages (rostbratwurst), approx. 3½oz (99,2) each
- 9oz (255g) ground beef
- 1 onion (finely diced)
- 7oz (198g) peppers in strips (frozen)
- 7oz (198g)Mushrooms (thinly sliced)
- 1 garlic clove
- 1 pack tomatoes, peeled (drained weight 8,5oz/240g)
- 1 pack tomatoes, strained (17,6oz/500g)
- low sodium salt and pepper
- paprika powder, hotter
- chili sauce, hot (from the Thai/Chinese store)
- 1 teaspoon butter

Cooking:
1. Saute the diced onions and bacon until translucent, then add the sliced grilled sausages and cook until lightly browned. Add the minced meat and cook until crumbly. After that, include the frozen pepper strips and mushroom slices, and let everything simmer for around 5 minutes.
2. Add the peeled tomatoes and the crushed tomatoes. Roughly chop the tomatoes with a spatula. Squeeze the garlic cloves and add them. Let the whole thing simmer for about 10 minutes.
3. Add salt, paprika, and hot chili sauce.
4. Pasta, rice, or a baguette with a nice salad taste great with it.

Nutrition Facts:
This recipe contains a good protein source, vitamins, and minerals.

Nutritional values per serving:
Calories 601 | Carbs 17g | Fat 45g (Trans 0g) | Sugar 7g | Fiber 2,6g |Sodium 990,2mg | Potassium 632,3mg | Cholesterol 50,4mg

Active: 20 min ¬ Total: 30 min¬ Serving: 4

TUSCANY MEATBALLS

The Italian herbs used in this recipe, chunky tomatoes, and mozzarella cheese give this dish a delicious flavor.

Ingredients:
- 1,1lb (499g) minced meat mixed
- possibly herbs (oregano, thyme, basil, etc.)
- possibly garlic
- 1 can tomatoes, chunky, about 1lb (454g)
- 3,5oz (99,2g) sweet cream
- 3 tbsp herbs, Italian (frozen)
- 1 tbsp tomato paste
- ½ tsp sugar (or sodium bicarbonate)
- 1 ball mozzarella
- low sodium salt and pepper

Cooking:
1. Add salt and pepper to the ground beef and herbs like oregano, thyme, basil, and Garlic if desired. Place the mixture into approximately 12-15 small balls in a casserole dish.
2. Combine the diced tomatoes, cream, herb mixture, tomato paste, and sugar for the tomato sauce.
3. Add salt and pepper to taste, then pour it over the meatballs in the casserole dish. Finally, slice the mozzarella and place it on top of the meatballs.
4. Cook in a hot oven at 175 °C for approx. 30 - 40 minutes. Be careful not to let the cheese get too dark.

Nutrition Facts:
Various herbs have antioxidant properties and may offer health benefits such as reducing inflammation.

Nutritional values per serving:
Sugar 3.7g | Fat 68.8g (Trans 0g)| Carbs: 19.5g | Calories 691 | Fiber 5,1g | Sodium 741,3mg | Potassium 1632,8mg | Cholesterol 80,4mg

Active: 30 min **Total:** 60 min **Serving:** 3

CAULIFLOWER STEAKS WITH LENTILS

Cauliflower steaks with lentils and plum sauce - This aroma miracle not only convinces vegetarians!

Ingredients:
- 5oz (141,7g) beluga lentils
- ½ tsp ground cumin
- 1 cauliflower
- ¼ tsp paprika powder
- ¼ tsp turmeric powder
- 7 plums
- 1 red onion
- 1 tbsp soy sauce
- dried thyme
- 1 tsp blue poppy

Cooking:
1. Boil lentils with water and cumin for 20 minutes.
2. Cut cauliflower into slices, coat with spices, and bake at 392°F (200°C) for 15-20 min.
3. Cut plums and onion, saute in oil and soy sauce for 5 min. Season with salt, pepper, and thyme.
4. Season lentils, add to plates with cauliflower, drizzle with plum sauce and sprinkle poppy seeds.

Nutrition Facts:
The ingredients are loaded with various B vitamins and vitamin C.

Nutritional values per serving:
Calories 283 | Fat 10g | Carbs 33g | Sugar 0g | Fiber 15,5g | Sodium 706mg | Potassium 1425,2mg | Cholesterol 0mg

Active: 20 min ¬ Total: 30 min ¬ Serving: 4

CURRIED CHICKEN STRIPS

A tasty second course low in calories and cholesterol and rich in amino acids.

Ingredients:
- 3-4 slices of chicken breast
- half of a leek
- half of an onion
- 1 leaf of sage
- 1 clove of garlic
- 2 mint leaves
- 2 tsp of curry powder
- rose salt
- half of liquid panna or cocoa milk
- coconut oil

Cooking:
1. Mince the leek, spring onion, sage, garlic, and saute them in a nonstick skillet with two tsp of coconut oil
2. Cut chicken slices into strips and toss them in curry
3. When the stir-fry is ready, add the meat and continue to cook over a low heat until the meat is golden brown
4. Add the cream or coconut milk and cook for 5/6 minutes more stirring all ingredients together

Nutrition Facts:
This dish provides a good amount of protein, fiber, and calcium.

Nutritional values per serving:
Carbohydrates 7,8g|Calories 449 cal|Sugar 1,08g|Fat 33.28g (Trans 0,1g)|Cholesterol 99 mg|Sodium 92 mg|Potassium 364,4 mg|Fiber 5,2g

Active: 15 min ¬ **Total:** 30 min ¬ **Serving:** 2

OVEN GNOCCHI IN A TOMATO AND PEPPER SAUCE

This is a good source of protein, carbohydrates and fat to help keep the body energized.

Ingredients:
- 17,6oz (499g) gnocchi
- 2 tbsp olive oil
- 1 garlic clove
- red pepper
- 17,6oz (499g) tomatoes, passed
- 7oz (198 g) cream cheese
- low sodium salt and pepper
- 1 bullet mozzarella
- 3,5oz (99,2) Parmesan
- oregano
- something broth granulated
- fat for the shape

Cooking:
1. Learn the peppers and puree them in a food processor. Peel the garlic clove, press, and saute in olive oil. Add the paprika puree and fry briefly. Add the tomato passata, stir in the cream cheese, and boil. Season to taste with salt, pepper, oregano, and broth.
2. Grease a casserole dish, spread the gnocchi, and pour the sauce. Cut the mozzarella into slices, grate the Parmesan, and distribute both on top.
3. Bake in a pre-heated oven at 180 °C for about 18 minutes.

Nutrition Facts:
The dish contains vitamins C, A, calcium, and iron.

Nutritional values per serving:
Calories: 667|Carbs 69g|Sugar: 4g|Fat: 32g (Trans 0g)|Fiber 9g|Sodium 1077 mg|Cholesterol 52 mg| Protein 68g

Active: 20 min ¬ **Total:** 40 min ¬ **Serving:** 3

STUFFED CELERY WITH CHEESE

The recipe is easy to make, which is a quick and tasty meal option.

Ingredients:
- 2 celeriac, peeled
- low sodium salt and pepper, white from the mill
- 1 teaspoon lemon juice
- 1 cheese, German Munster cheese (small loaf 5,3oz/150g)
- 1 tbsp wholemeal flour
- 1 egg, whisked
- 6 tbsp breadcrumbs
- 2 tbsp clarified butter

Cooking:
1. Boil the celery in salted water until al dente. Cut each bulb crosswise into 4 slices, season with salt and pepper, and sprinkle with lemon juice.
2. Also, cut the Munster cheese into 4 slices and place each between 2 slices of celery.
3. Roll stuffed celery in flour, then egg, then breadcrumbs, pressing well
4. Then fry the celery slices in clarified butter until golden brown.

Nutrition Facts:
The ingredients contain fiber and vitamins, including vitamins K and C.

Nutritional values per serving:
Calories: 363 cal|Fat: 16,1g (Trans 0g)|Carbs: 23g|Sugar 5g|Sodium 280,7-Potassium 375,9| Cholesterol 28,3g|Fiber 2g

Active: 30 min ¬ **Total:** 40 min ¬ **Serving:** 4

APRICOT BREAD WITH CREAM CHEESE

Apricot bread with cream cheese. Quickly made gourmet delights for in-between!

Ingredients:
- 4 apricots
- ½ vanilla bean
- 1 tsp honey
- 2 discs wholemeal rye bread
- 1oz (28g) goat cream cheese
- low sodium salt
- pepper
- 1 branch rosemary

Cooking:
1. Cut the apricots into wedges after washing and removing the pits. Combine honey, apricots, and scraped vanilla pulp from half a vanilla pod in a pot. Cook the mixture over low heat for 3 minutes.
2. Spread goat's cream cheese on both slices of bread and season with salt and pepper. Top the bread with apricot wedges and sprinkle with washed and dried rosemary needles. Serve.

Nutrition Facts:
Plenty of potassium from the apricots helps gently rid the body of excess water retention. Carotenoids and vitamins C and E support the immune system.

Nutritional values per serving:
Calories 175 | Fat 3g (Trans 0g) | Carbs 31g | Sugar 2.6g | Fiber 4,8g | Sodium 88,1mg | Potassium 1074,1mg | Cholesterol 0mg

Active: 40 min ¬ **Total:** 60 min ¬ **Serving:** 2

PAPRIKA RICE PAN WITH YOGURT SAUCE

Perfect dish for energy.

Ingredients:
- 2 cups brown rice
- 4 cups vegetable broth

For the vegetables:
- 2 onions
- 2 toes of garlic
- 1 chili pepper
- 3 tbsp tomato paste
- 3 bell peppers, as mixed as you like
- 1 teaspoon paprika powder, rose-spicy
- 1 handful of herbs, mixed (basil and parsley), fresh
- 1 teaspoon paprika powder, noble sweet

For the sauce:
- 10,5oz nonfat yogurt (298g)
- 2 tsp of garlic
- low sodium salt and pepper

Cooking:
1. Cook the rice in vegetable broth using a measuring cup of approximately 200-250 ml.
2. Dice the peppers and finely chop the onions. In a pan, sauté the onions in a little oil until translucent, then add the pressed garlic, chili pepper, and tomato paste and saute briefly. Add the diced peppers to the pan and sauté for a few minutes, tossing the pan occasionally. Season with paprika, salt, and pepper. Add the rice, mix it in, and let it heat up. Finally, chop the herbs and mix them in. Taste and adjust seasoning.
3. Mix the yogurt and pressed garlic, and season with salt and pepper. Serve the rice with a dollop of the yogurt sauce.
4. This amount can feed around 3-4 people, and the rice can also be served as a side dish.
5. Feel free to add more herbs according to your preference.

Nutrition Facts:
This recipe contains vitamins, minerals, and antioxidants.

Nutritional values per serving:
Calories:375 cal|Carbs 78,8g|Sugar 3g|Fat 6,4g (Trans 0g)|Sodium 773,3 mg|Cholesterol 4,9 mg|Fiber 1,6g|Potassium 624,8 g

Active: 30 min ¬ **Total:** 50 min ¬ **Serving:** 4

BRITTA'S ROBBER MEAT

It is a versatile meal option that can be served with a variety of sides.

Ingredients:
- 4 pork schnitzel or chicken, turkey
- 1 onion
- 1 pack of bacon cubes
- 1 package of mushrooms, approx. 10,5oz (298g) cut into thin slices
- 2 pickled cucumber
- 2 bell pepper
- 2 toes garlic
- 8½floz (251ml) broth
- 1 sour mug of cream, approx. 7oz (198g)
- 2 tbsp tomato paste
- tabasco
- low sodium salt and pepper
- paprika powder, rose-spicy

Cooking:
1. Season the schnitzel in a casserole dish with salt and pepper.
2. In a lightly greased pan, fry the onion. Add the bacon, mushrooms, gherkins, and paprika, and saute briefly. Add the pressed garlic, pour in the broth, and stir in the sour cream and tomato paste. Season the sauce with hot pepper sauce, salt, and paprika powder. Pour the sauce over the schnitzels into the casserole dish.
3. Cook in a hot oven at 338°F (170 °C) circulating air or 392°F (200 °C) top/bottom heat for approx. 20 to 30 minutes - depending on the meat.
4. This goes well with bread, pasta, rice, and much more.

Nutrition Facts:
Good source of potassium and vitamin C

Nutritional values per serving:
Calories 556 kcal | Carbs 23.4g | Fat 71.3g (Trans 0g) | Sugar 4.7g | Fiber 8g | Sodium 76,2mg | Potassium 580,5mg | Cholesterol 0mg

Active: 40 min ¬ **Total:** 60 min ¬ **Serving:** 4

FETA CHEESE ON CAULIFLOWER RICE

Sheep's cheese from the oven on cauliflower rice. Creamy, crunchy, and super healthy.

Ingredients:
- 14oz (397g) feta cheese (9% fat)
- 3 tbsp hazelnuts
- 1 carrot
- ½ red onion
- 1lb (454g) small cauliflower
- 1 bunch Parsley
- 1 tsp lemon juice

Cooking:
1. Cut sheep's cheese into four pieces and place in a casserole dish. Roughly chop the hazelnuts. Clean, wash and coarsely grate the carrots. Peel and chop the onion. Mix the nuts with the carrot, onion, and oil, and season with salt and pepper. Spread the mix over the cheese and bake in a preheated oven at 392°F(200°C) (356°F/180°C fan oven, gas: level 3) for 10 minutes.
2. Meanwhile, trim and wash the cauliflower, cut it into quarters, and grate coarsely. Wash the parsley, shake dry, and chop. Mix cauliflower with parsley and lemon juice and season with salt and pepper. Then serve the cauliflower rice with the feta cheese.

Nutrition Facts:

Cauliflower is a low-calorie, low-carb substitute for rice. It scores with lots of vitamin C and lots of minerals. With the feta cheese and the nuts, high-quality proteins and good fats come into play.

Nutritional values per serving:

Calories 293 | Fat 18g | Carbs 8g | Sugar 0g | Fiber 3,0g | Sodium 140mg | Potassium 928,6mg | Cholesterol 14.7mg

Active: 20 min ¬ **Total:** 30 min ¬ **Serving:** 4

CAULIFLOWER STEAKS WITH LENTILS

Vegetable and lentil stew with peas. Filling soup for spooning.

Ingredients:
- 0,2oz (5,7g) ginger root
- 1 shallot
- 1 sweet potato
- 3½oz (99,2) celery root
- 2,8oz (79,3g) red lenses
- 1 tsp harissa paste
- 1 tbsp tomato paste
- ½ tsp curry powder
- 20 floz (591ml) vegetable broth
- 4 tbsp coconut milk
- 2 pieces spring onions
- 5,3oz (150g) frozen peas
- 2 tsp sunflower seeds

Cooking:
1. Begin by peeling and chopping the ginger and shallot. Cut the sweet potato and celery into small cubes after washing and peeling them.
1. Saute ginger, shallot, sweet potato, and celery in 1 tablespoon of oil for 5 minutes in a saucepan. Add lentils, harissa, tomato paste, and curry powder, and saute for another 4 minutes.
2. Season the mixture with salt, pepper, and vegetable stock and simmer for 15 minutes. Stir in 2 tablespoons of coconut milk.
3. Saute spring onions, peas, and sunflower seeds in the remaining oil for 5 minutes. Pour soup into two bowls, top the mixture, and drizzle with the remaining coconut milk.

Nutrition Facts:

Vegetables provide a lot of dietary fiber, which promotes digestion, and a lot of potassium, which regulates blood pressure.

Nutritional values per serving:

Calories 592 | Fat 23g (Trans 0g) | Carbs 74g | Sugar 0g | Fiber 18,1g | Sodium 300,7mg | Potassium 994,6mg | Cholesterol 176,7mg

Active: 20 min ¬ **Total:** 30 min ¬ **Serving:** 2

STUFFED SALMON TROUT FILLETS

Aromatic, light fish enjoyment with Italian overtones

Ingredients:
- 1,7oz (48g) sun-dried tomatoes
- 2lb (907g) large salmon trout fillet
- low sodium salt
- pepper
- 2 tbsp grainy mustard
- 2 organic limes
- 1 bunch Arugula
- 3 stems basil

Cooking:
1. Take a small bowl and place the tomatoes in it. Cover the tomatoes with hot water and let them soak for 10 minutes. Drain the tomatoes in a sieve, squeeze the excess water, and chop them coarsely.
2. While the tomatoes are soaking, wash the fish fillets and pat them dry using paper towels. Season the meat sides with salt and pepper and brush them lightly with mustard.
3. Rinse the limes under hot water, dry them, and slice them thinly.
4. Trim, wash, and dry the arugula. Wash the basil, shake the excess water, and pluck off the leaves. Using a large knife, roughly chop the arugula and basil and place them in a bowl.
5. Mix the tomatoes and olive oil with the herbs until well combined. Spread this mixture on the flesh sides of the salmon trout fillets.
6. Place the fillets carefully on each other, fleshy sides together, and tie them loosely with kitchen twine.
7. Spread half of the lime slices in a casserole dish. Place the fish on top of the lime slices with the remaining lime slices, and bake in a preheated oven at 200 °C (180 °C fan oven, gas level 3) for 15-20 minutes.

Nutrition Facts:

The fillet contains a good portion of valuable unsaturated fatty acids, but it remains extremely low in fat thanks to how it is prepared.

Nutritional values per serving:

Calories 345 | Fat 9g (Trans 0g) | Carbs 6g | Sugar 0g | Fiber 4,8g | Sodium 62,7mg | Potassium 708,1mg | Cholesterol 97,3mg

Active: 20 min ¬ **Total:** 40 min ¬ **Serving:** 4

VEGETARIAN CHICKPEA CURRY WITH APRICOTS

Aromatic treat.

Ingredients:
- 6,3oz (178g) brown rice
- low sodium salt
- 1,3lb (590g) tomatoes
- 2 onions
- 0,3oz (8,5g) ginger
- 1 clove of garlic
- 3½oz (99,2) dried apricots
- 1 oz (28g) clarified butter
- 9,3oz (264g) chickpeas
- cinnamon
- ground cardamom
- 2 tsp garam masala
- 4 stems coriander
- 1,6oz (45g) cashew nuts
- 4,4oz (125g) sheep's milk yogurt

Cooking:
1. Cook the rice in 2½ cups salt water per packet directions.
2. In the meantime, wash the tomatoes and score them with a kitchen knife. Immerse in boiling water for a few seconds, remove, rinse and peel.
3. Quarter the tomatoes, remove the seeds, and roughly puree the flesh.
4. Peel onions, ginger, and Garlic. Cut onions into fine rings. Finely chop the Garlic and ginger. Cut the apricots into fine strips.
5. Heat butter in a saucepan. Add onions, ginger, and apricots and sauté over medium heat for 3-5 minutes until translucent.
6. Rinse the chickpeas, drain, and add to the onion and apricot mix with the Garlic, tomato puree, cinnamon, cardamom, garam masala, salt, and 100 ml water. Simmer the chickpea curry over low heat for about 5 minutes.
7. Meanwhile, wash the coriander, shake it dry, pluck off the leaves, and roughly chop. Roughly chop the cashew nuts as well. Serve the chickpea curry with basmati rice and sheep's yogurt and garnish with coriander and cashew nuts.

Nutrition Facts:
The Cashew nuts have a lot of magnesium to offer, which allows us to keep a cool head in stressful situations.

Nutritional values per serving:
Calories 639 | Protein 20g| Fat 21g (Trans 0g) | Carbs 88g| Sugar 0g | Fiber 2,8g | Sodium 457,9mg | Potassium 1056,9mg | Cholesterol 0g

Active: 20 min ¬ **Total:** 50 min ¬ **Serving:** 3

SALMON FILLET WITH PEPPERS

This delicious omega-3 supplier tastes great for young and old.

Ingredients:
- 3 peppers
- 1 clove of garlic
- 1 shallot
- 2 salmon fillets
- 1 piece ginger
- dried thyme
- low sodium salt
- 1,7oz (48ml) vegetable broth
- 3½ (99g) couscous

Cooking:
1. Start by washing the peppers, then cut them in half, remove the seeds, and cut them into strips. Finely chop the garlic and shallot after peeling them. Rinse the salmon fillets under cold water, pat them dry, and cut them into cubes. Peel and grate the ginger.
2. In a large non-stick skillet, heat 1 tablespoon oil. Fry the salmon cubes with the garlic, shallot, and ginger over medium heat until they turn golden brown on all sides. Remove them from the pan and set them aside.
3. Using the same pan, heat the remaining oil over medium heat. Add the pepper strips and saute them for 2-3 minutes. Season them with thyme, salt, and pepper, then deglaze the pan by pouring in the broth. Let the mixture simmer, stirring occasionally, until almost all the liquid has evaporated, which should take around 5 minutes.
4. Meanwhile, pour twice the amount of boiling salted water over the couscous and let it steep for 5 minutes.

Nutrition Facts:

Salmon provides many omega-3 fatty acids, which have an anti-inflammatory effect. The peppers are a real vitamin C bomb.

Nutritional values per serving:

Calories 569 | Fat 24g | Carbs 55g | Sugar 0g (Trans og) | Fiber 0g | Sodium 135,4 mg | Potassium 1095,4mg | Cholesterol 120mg

Active: 20 min ¬ **Total:** 30 min ¬ **Serving:** 2

TROUT FILLETS

Trout fillets with an herb crust, carrots, parsnips, and vegetables. Tender fish with crunchy vegetables. A successful contrast.

Ingredients:
- 4 trout fillets
- low sodium salt
- pepper
- organic lime
- 1,4oz (40g) pine nuts
- 0,35oz (10g) parsley
- 0,35oz (10g) mint
- 1 slice wholemeal toast
- 4 carrots
- parsnips
- 0,17oz (4,8g) ginger root
- ½ tbsp honey

Cooking:
1. Wash the trout fillets and pat dry. Heat 2 tablespoons of olive oil on a skillet. Sear the fillets over medium heat for 10-15 seconds on each side. Remove, lightly salt and pepper, and set aside.
2. Squeeze the lime juice. Roast the pine nuts in a hot pan without fat, remove, and let cool.
3. Meanwhile, wash the herbs, shake them dry, pluck off the leaves, and set aside a few mint leaves. Finely chop the toast and herbs and mix everything with 1 tbsp olive oil and 2 tbsp lime juice. Roughly chop half of the pine nuts.
4. Clean the carrots and parsnips, peel, and cut lengthwise into fine strips. Ginger peel and finely chop.
5. Heat the rest of the olive oil in a frying pan. Fry the vegetable strips over medium heat for 10 minutes. Then add ginger and honey and let caramelize for 3 minutes. Salt.
6. While the vegetable strips are roasting, spread the herb crust over the trout fillets and cook at 220 °C (convection oven 200 °C; gas: level 3-4) for 10 minutes.

Nutrition Facts:
This dish is rich in healthy fats, iron, and omega-3.

Nutritional values per serving:
Calories 379 | Fat 20g (Trans 0,9g) | Carbs 17g | Sugar 1g | Fiber 1,1g | Sodium 48,2mg | Potassium 431,9mg | Cholesterol 138,2mg

Active: 40 min ¬ **Total:** 60 min ¬ **Serving:** 4

TOMATO SALMON

Tender fish with fruity vegetables.

Ingredients:
- 2,2lb (998g) cocktail tomatoes
- 3 garlic cloves
- 2 red peppers
- 3 tbsp olive oil
- 5,3oz (150g) black olives
- 1oz (28g) capers
- 5 tbsp lemon juice
- low sodium salt
- pepper
- 1 tbsp honey
- 1,4lb (635g) salmon fillet (8 salmon fillets)
- 0,3oz (8,5g) parsley

Cooking:
1. Start by washing and quartering the tomatoes. Peel and slice the garlic, and halve the peppers lengthwise, removing the seeds and cutting them into rings. Heat some olive oil over medium-high heat in a large pan, and saute the tomatoes for about 3 minutes, stirring occasionally.
2. To the tomatoes, add the garlic, pepperoni, olives, and capers, and saute over medium heat for 5 minutes. Then pour 200 ml of water and let the mixture simmer for 7 minutes over low heat.
3. Squeeze lemon juice over the tomatoes and season with salt, pepper, and honey.
4. Rinse the salmon pieces and place them on top of the tomatoes. Cover and cook for 5 minutes.
5. Remove the pan from the heat. Let stand for 4 minutes. In the meantime, wash the parsley, shake it dry, and chop the leaves. Sprinkle the parsley over the salmon before serving.

Nutrition Facts:
This dish is a rich source of vitamin A, healthy fats, and Omega-6.

Nutritional values per serving:
Calories 488 | Fat 33g (Trans 0g) | Carbs 48g | Sugar 4g | Fiber 4,2g | Sodium 485,5mg | Potassium 915,2mg | Cholesterol 52,2mg

Active: 20 min ¬ **Total:** 40 min ¬ **Serving:** 4

OVEN VEGETABLES

Quick and easy and super tasty

Ingredients:
- 1,1lb (499g) potatoes
- 0,9lb (408g) pointed pepper, red
- thyme
- marjoram
- oregano
- rosemary
- 5,2oz (147g) cherry tomatoes
- 7oz (198 g) mushrooms
- 3½oz (99g) feta cheese
- 1 onion
- 6 garlic cloves
- sea salt and pepper
- caraway seeds
- paprika powder, rose-spicy

Cooking:
1. Preheat the oven to 200 °C top/bottom heat.
2. Heat a pan with plenty of good olive oil. Halve the washed and peeled potatoes and toss briefly in the pan. Halve the pointed peppers, deseed, cut them into small pieces, and add briefly. Mix everything with the herbs and place in an ovenproof dish.
3. Quarter the cherry tomatoes, halve the mushrooms, and dice the feta cheese. Cut the onion into rings and peel the Garlic (possibly use more or less Garlic, but this type of preparation does not leave an extreme garlic taste). Put all these ingredients in the dish, stir, and season with sea salt, pepper, cumin, and hot paprika powder.
4. Put in the preheated oven and bake for about 30 minutes.
5. When the potatoes are soft, you can serve them.

Nutrition Facts:

Rich with fibers, vitamins and minerals, it is a healthy and nutritious choice.

Nutritional values per serving:

Calories 300 | Fat 15g (Trans 0g) | Carbs 30g | Sugar 5g | Fiber 13,3g | Sodium 194,5mg | Potassium 1087,3mg | Cholesterol 0mg

Active: 40 min ¬ **Total:** 60 min ¬ **Serving:** 2

LEMONY FISH FILLET WITH ZUCCHINI VEGETABLES

Healthy all around: fixed pan with a fresh, fruity aroma

Ingredients:
- 1,3lb (590g) fish fillet
- 2 zucchini
- 4 spring onions
- 1 organic lemon
- 4 stems of parsley
- low sodium salt
- pepper
- 3,4floz (100ml) fish stock

Cooking:
1. Start by rinsing the fish with cold water and drying it off. Then proceed to wash, trim, and finely dice the courgettes. Next, wash and trim the spring onions and cut them into rings. Rinse the lemon with hot water, dry it, peel off the zest, and squeeze out the juice. Lastly, wash the parsley, shake it dry, and chop the leaves.
2. Heat 1 tablespoon of the oil and sauté the spring onions and zucchini over a medium heat for 2 to 3 minutes. Once cooked, remove it from the heat, season the mixture with salt and pepper, and let it simmer.
3. While the courgettes and spring onions are simmering, heat the remaining oil in another pan and fry the fish fillets until golden brown, which should take around 2 minutes per side. Salt and pepper the fillets and place on the zucchini mixture.
4. Deglaze the fish roast with the fish stock and let it simmer briefly. Add lemon juice to taste and the lemon zest, and season with salt and pepper. Finally, add the chopped parsley and drizzle the sauce over the fillets.

Nutrition Facts:
As well as plenty of protein, this tender seafood contains lots of iodine, which is important for the thyroid.

Nutritional values per serving:
Calories 235 | Fat 9g (Trans 0g) | Carbs 4g | Sugar 0g | Fiber 4,7g | Sodium 69mg | Potassium 542,3mg | Cholesterol 57,7mg

Active: 10 min ¬ **Total:** 30 min ¬ **Serving:** 4

RUTABAGA AND MASHED POTATOES

Lukewarm smoked fish on earthy mash with many onions.

Ingredients:
- 1,1lb(499g) swede
- 5floz (148ml) classic vegetable broth
- 1½lb (580g) floury potatoes
- 10,5oz (298g) red onions
- 1 tbsp rapeseed oil
- 7oz (198g) smoked trout fillet
- ½ bunch chervil
- ½ bunch dill
- 3,4floz (100ml) milk (3.5% fat)
- low sodium salt
- pepper
- nutmeg

Cooking:
1. Wash the swede, peel it, and cut it into small cubes.
2. Start by heating a saucepan and boiling the vegetable broth. Once boiling, add the diced turnips and let them cook for around 8 minutes over low heat while covered.
3. While the turnips are cooking, peel the potatoes, rinse them thoroughly, and cut them into cubes about 2 cm in size. Add the potatoes to the turnips and cook them covered over low heat for 20 more minutes.
4. While the Swedes and potatoes are cooking, peel and halve the onions and slice them into thin rings.
5. Take a non-stick pan and heat some rapeseed oil in it. Add the sliced onions and fry them over low heat for 8-12 minutes, turning them frequently.
6. To prepare the trout fillets, place them on a large sheet of baking paper. Loosely fold the paper to create a packet, then place it on a baking tray. Preheat the oven to 100°C and bake the trout for approximately 10 minutes. Rinse the chervil and dill and shake dry. Pluck the dill and chervil into small sprigs, set aside some, and roughly chop the rest.
7. Boil the milk in a small saucepan. Mash the cooked swede and potato cubes with a potato masher, gradually adding the hot milk.
8. Salt and pepper the puree. Grate in some nutmeg and fold in with the chopped herbs.
9. Season the fried onion rings with a little salt and pour over the puree. Garnish with sprigs of dill and chervil. Unwrap the warmed trout fillets, cut them in half, and serve with them.

Nutrition Facts:
One serving provides twice the daily requirement of vitamin D.

Nutritional values per serving:
Calories 233 | Fat 6g (Trans 0,2g) | Carbs 28g | Sugar 0g | Fiber 4,6g | Sodium 62,5mg | Potassium 601mg | Cholesterol 0mg

Active: 50 min ¬ **Total:** 60 min ¬ **Serving:** 4

STEWED CUCUMBERS WITH SALMON AND DILL

Low-carb enjoyment on the fly: tender salmon in a creamy sauce.

Ingredients:
- 1,1lb (499g) cucumber
- 1 red onion
- 8,8oz (249g) salmon fillet
- low sodium salt
- pepper
- 0,3floz (8,9ml) classic vegetable broth
- 0,3oz (8,5g) sour cream (10% fat)
- 1 bunch of dill
- 2 tbsp sunflower seeds oil

Cooking:
1. Rinse the salmon fillet, pat dry, and cut it into 2 cm cubes. Heat oil in skillet and fry fish over medium heat until lightly browned, 4 minutes   Remove salt and pepper.
2. Heat a pan and add diced onion. Sauté over medium-high heat for 2 minutes. Next, add cucumbers and saute for an additional 2 minutes. Season the mixture with salt and pepper.
3. Pour in the broth and sour cream and bring it to a brief boil. Reduce heat and let simmer for 4-5 minutes.
4. While the mixture is simmering, prepare the dill by washing, shaking, drying, and chopping it. Return salmon to pan and cook another 2 minutes. Don't forget to season it with salt and pepper. To serve, sprinkle the dish with dill and sunflower seeds.

Nutrition Facts:
In combination with olive oil and sunflower seeds, valuable fats are combined in this dish.

Nutritional values per serving:
Calories 527 | Fat 38g (Trans 0g) | Carbs 14g | Sugar 0g | Fiber 8,5g | Sodium 62,9mg | Potassium 708,1mg | Cholesterol 34,4mg

Active: 10 min ¬ **Total:** 20 min ¬ **Serving:** 2

POTATO CHICKEN BREAST

Heaven and Earth. This healthy alternative is also a visual treat!

Ingredients:
- 1,7lb (771g) floury potatoes
- low sodium salt
- 0,9lb (408g) chicken breast fillet
- 3½ tbsp rapeseed oil
- 1 tbsp lemon juice
- 2 onions
- 1 handful of herbs (parsley, dill, chives)
- 2 spring onions
- 0,7oz (20g) hazelnuts
- 6,7floz (198ml) hot milk (3.5% fat)
- 1 tbsp clarified butter
- nutmeg
- 3 apples

Cooking:
1. Clean the potatoes and place them in a pot with their skins on. Cover them with cold water, add salt, and bring them to a boil. Cook on medium heat for 25 minutes, then drain and allow the steam to evaporate.
2. Next, slice the chicken breast fillet into 3 cm long strips. Mix 2 tbsp of oil with 1 tbsp of lemon juice, add salt and pepper, then coat the meat with the marinade. Cover and refrigerate for 20 minutes while you work on other steps.
3. Peel the onions, slice them into rings, and saute in a pan with 1 tbsp of oil over medium heat for 3-5 minutes, stirring occasionally. Season with salt, then drain on kitchen paper.
4. Finely chop the washed herbs, cut the spring onions into diagonal rings, and coarsely chop the hazelnuts. Peel and mash the potatoes, stir in hot milk and butter, then season the puree with nutmeg, salt, and pepper.
5. Wash and wedge the apples, removing the core. Heat a grill pan, brush with ½ tbsp oil, and grill the apple slices over low heat for 2-3 minutes on each side. Then grill the marinated chicken in the same pan for 3-4 minutes over medium heat, turning as needed.
6. Spread the mashed potatoes on 4 plates, and arrange the chicken breast strips, apple slices, and onion rings on top. Serve sprinkled with herbs, spring onions, and hazelnuts.

Nutrition Facts:

Chicken breast fillet it's low in fat, rich in protein, and provides nerve and muscle-strengthening magnesium.

Nutritional values per serving:

Calories 524 | Fat 18g (Trans 1,2g) | Carbs 58g | Sugar 0g | Fiber 2,3g | 91,8mg | Potassium 423,2mg | Cholesterol 86,1mg

Active: 50 min ¬ **Total:** 60 min ¬ **Serving:** 4

MARINATED TOFU

A bowl full of healthy delicacies

Ingredients:
- 0,9lb (408g) tofu
- 1 clove of garlic
- 1 tbsp sesame oil
- 1 pinch sambal oelek
- 2 tbsp teriyaki sauce
- 5,3oz (150g) red cabbage
- low sodium salt
- pepper
- 2 kohlrabi
- 1 carrot
- 2 tbsp apple cider vinegar
- 1 tbsp honey
- 1 tbsp lemon juice
- 1 tsp mustard
- ½ tsp thyme
- ¼ tsp turmeric powder
- 4 stems parsley
- 15g sesame (1 tbsp)

Cooking:
1. Cut tofu into 8 slices. Peel and chop the Garlic and mix with sesame oil and teriyaki sauce. Marinate the tofu with it and let it stand for 20 minutes.
2. While waiting, take the red cabbage, wash it, and slice it into thin pieces. Add salt and pepper, and use your hands to knead it for about 5 minutes until it becomes soft. Wash the kohlrabi and carrot, grate them, and mix them.
3. Add olive oil, vinegar, honey, lemon juice, and mustard to create the dressing. Add thyme, turmeric, salt, and pepper for seasoning.
4. Drain the tofu a little, place it in a hot pan, and fry it for 4 minutes on each side over medium heat. Pour marinade over tofu and simmer for 2 minutes. Season it with salt and pepper. Wash the parsley, shake it dry, and chop it. Serve the kohlrabi and carrot mixed with red cabbage and tofu. Drizzle with the dressing, and sprinkle with sesame seeds and parsley.

Nutrition Facts:
Curcumin gives the dressing a beautiful color and has an anti-inflammatory effect.

Nutritional values per serving:
Calorie 287 | Fat 18g (Trans 0g) | Carbs 12g | Sugar 0g | Fiber 5,0g | Sodium 101mg | Potassium 813,6mg | Cholesterol 0mg

Active: 40 min ¬ **Total:** 60 min ¬ **Serving:** 4

ORANGE SALMON WITH NUT RICE

Healthy soul food from the oven

Ingredients:
- 8,8oz (249g) basmati brown rice
- low sodium salt
- 1 organic orange
- 1,4oz (40g) herbs (1 handful; of parsley and dill)
- 5 tbsp extr virgin olive oil
- pepper
- 1,3lb (590g) salmon fillet (4 salmon fillets)
- 1,7oz (48g) salted cashew nuts

Cooking:
1. Cook the rice in salted water according to the instructions on the packet until it is al dente.
2. Wash the orange in hot water and pat dry while the rice cooks. Grate the zest finely. Squeeze out the juice. Mix with 4 tbsp olive oil, salt and pepper. Grease a casserole dish with the rest of the oil. Rinse the salmon under cold water. Pat dry and brush with the marinade.
3. Chop the nuts. Pour boiled rice into bowl, sprinkle with nuts and top with salmon fillet. Heat in the oven for about 20 minutes at 392°F/200°C (356°F/180°C fan, gas mark3).

Nutrition Facts:

Brown rice contains vitamins and minerals and provides a lot of filling fiber. The nuts contains protein and good fatty acid composition.

Nutritional values per serving:

Calories 689 | Fat 37g | Carbs 52g| Fat 7,1g (Trans 0g) | Sugar 0g | Fiber 8,5g | Sodium 62,7mg | Potassium 712,6mg | Cholesterol 34,4mg

Active: 20 min ¬ **Total:** 60 min¬ **Serving:** 4

SALMON SPINACH PASTA

Delicious pasta dish with fresh lemon.

Ingredients:
- 1,1lb (499g) wholemeal pasta (e.g., penne)
- 1 clove of garlic
- 1 red onion
- 1 organic lemon
- 10floz (296ml) vegetable broth
- 3 tbsp cream cheese
- 8,8oz (249g) salmon fillet
- 2,8oz (79g) spinach
- pepper

Cooking:
1. Cook noodles as per package instructions and drain.
2. Peel and dice garlic and onion. Rinse and grate the lemon zest.
3. Saute garlic and onion in oil. Add lemon zest and vegetable broth.
4. Cut salmon fillet, add to the sauce, and let it simmer for 5 minutes.
5. Wash and spin dry the spinach. Add to the salmon with the noodles, season with pepper, and mix well. Divide the salmon pasta with spinach among four plates and serve.

Nutrition Facts:

The tender salmon contains protein and healthy, polyunsaturated fatty acids.

Nutritional values per serving:

Calories 612 | Fat 18g (Trans 0g) | Carbs 58g | Sugar 0g | Fiber 3,7g | Sodium 122,9mg | Potassium 332mg | Cholesterol 22,5mg

Active: 10 min ¬ **Total:** 20 min ¬ **Serving:**

SESAME-CRUSTED SALMON AND BROCCOLI

Tender fish with an aromatic crust and crunchy vegetables

Ingredients:
- 1,3lb (590g) broccoli
- low sodium salt
- 1 clove of garlic
- ½oz (14g) ginger
- 1lb (453g) very fresh salmon fillet (8 pieces)
- pepper
- 1oz (28g) sesame
- 1 tbsp coconut oil
- 2 tbsp sesame oil
- chili threads
- 1,7floz (50ml) vegetable broth
- 2 tbsp lime juice
- 1 ime

Cooking:
1. Cut broccoli into small florets. Boil the florets in salted water for four minutes before draining, rinsing, and ensuring they are well drained. While the broccoli is cooking, finely chop the garlic, peel, and grate the ginger. Rinse the salmon with cold water, pat it dry, and season it with salt and pepper. Coat the salmon with sesame seeds.
2. To fry the salmon, heat some coconut oil in a pan and place the salmon in the pan with the skin side down. Flip it over until the skin side is golden brown, and fry the other side until golden brown. Once it is cooked, transfer the salmon to an ovenproof plate or baking tray, and keep it warm in a preheated oven at 100°C (not recommended for convection ovens; if using gas, use the lowest setting) for about 10 minutes. The salmon should still be slightly translucent on the inside.
3. While the salmon is in the oven, heat some sesame oil in a wok, and saute the garlic and ginger. Add the broccoli and chili threads, and mix them in. Then, deglaze the wok with broth, season with salt, pepper, and lime juice, and garnish with lime wedges. Rinse the lime with hot water, dry it, and cut it into wedges.

Nutrition Facts:

Salmon is high in healthy omega-3s. These polyunsaturated fatty acids can improve concentration and memory, among other things.

Nutritional values per serving:

Calories 393 | Fat 27g (Trans 0,2g) | Carbs 6g | Sugar 0g | Fiber 6,8g | Sodium 369,4mg | Potassium 944,7mg | Cholesterol 28mg

Active: 20 min ¬ **Total:** 30 min ¬ **Serving:** 4

SALMON MEATBALLS ON LEEKS

Protein-rich fish patties with crunchy, creamy leeks.

Ingredients:
- 1oz (28g) onions
- 1,3lb (590g) salmon fillet
- 4 stems dill
- 1 egg
- 1 tsp mustard
- 1,7oz (48g) wholemeal breadcrumbs
- sea salt
- pepper
- 2 bars leek
- 2 tbsp rapeseed oil
- 1,7oz (48g) cream cheese (45% fat in dry matter)
- ¼ tsp ground cumin
- ¼ tsp dried marjoram

Cooking:
1. Wash and chop the dill. Knead the salmon with onion, half of the dill, egg, mustard, breadcrumbs, salt, and pepper into a malleable mass. Shape the mixture into 8-12 meatballs, depending on their size.
2. In a large skillet, heat the olive oil over a medium-high heat. Cook the meatballs for approximately 5 minutes per side.
3. At the same time, clean the leeks, wash them thoroughly, and cut them into rings. Heat the remaining oil in a pan. Sauté the leeks in it over medium heat for 5 minutes. Add cream cheese and 3-4 tbsp water and stir until creamy.
4. Arrange the salmon meatballs on the leeks and decorate them with the remaining dill.

Nutrition Facts:
Salmon meatballs are rich in animal protein and valuable omega-3 fatty acids.

Nutritional values per serving:
Calories 439 | Fat 28g (Trans 0g) | Carbs 11g | Sugar 0g | Fiber 0,7g | Sodium 140,4mg | Potassium 712,2mg | Cholesterol 34,4 mg

Active: 20 min ¬ **Total:** 30 min ¬ **Serving:** 4

TARTE FLAMBEE WITH BEETROOT

Tarte flambe with beetroot and plums. Soul food for autumn.

Ingredients:
- 0,9lb (408g) spelled flour type 1050
- 1 packet of dry yeast
- low sodium salt
- 1,7oz (48g) avogado pulp
- 1 tsp honey
- 2 branches of thyme
- 7oz (198g) goat cream cheese
- pepper
- 2 beetroot
- 2 spring onions
- 4 red plums
- 3½oz (99g) halloumi
- 1,7oz (48g) walnut kernels
- 4 tbsp rapeseed oil

Cooking:
1. Mix flour, yeast, salt, margarine, honey, and water to make dough. Let it rise for 1 hour.
2. Roll dough into 4 flatbreads and put them on baking trays with paper.
3. Mix half the thyme with goat's cheese, and slice beetroot, spring onions, plums, cheese, and walnuts. Apply cheese to flat breads and add vegetables and cheese. Bake at 220°C for 15-20 minutes. Top with remaining thyme, walnuts, pepper, and rapeseed oil.

Nutrition Facts:
The secondary plant substances betaine and anthocyanins from beetroot and plums are anti-inflammatory and protect our cells.

Nutritional values per serving:
Calories 859 | Fat 47g (Trans 0g) | Carbs 81g | Sugar 1g | Cholesterol 0g | Fiber 3,2g | Sodium 51,1mg | Potassium 526,1

Active: 40 min ¬ **Total:** 100 min ¬ **Serving:** 4

TAGLIATELLE AND MARINATED SALMON

Raw fish on warm pasta.

Ingredients:
- 1 tbsp pine nuts
- 1oz (28g) pecorino
- 2,8oz (79g) rocket (1 bunch)
- 4 cherry tomatoes
- ½ lime
- 7oz (198g) salmon fillet (very fresh; sushi quality)
- low sodium salt
- pepper
- 10½oz (297g) fresh pasta

Cooking:
1. Toast the nuts and let them cool down.
2. Finely grate the Pecorino with a vegetable peeler.
3. Rinse half a lime in hot water, rub dry, and finely grate the zest. Squeeze Lime.
4. Rinse the salmon fillet, pat dry with kitchen paper, and cut it into wafer-thin slices.
5. Put the salmon in a bowl, and add the salt, pepper, lime juice, and zest. Mix everything well and leave covered in the fridge (marinate).
6. Meanwhile, bring 3 liters of lightly salted water to a boil in a large saucepan. Cook the Tagliatelle according to the instructions on the packet, drain in a sieve and allow to drain.
7. When the noodles are cooked, transfer them to a heated bowl and combine them with the tomatoes, rocket, sliced salmon, chili, and olive oil. Add salt and pepper to taste. If needed, quickly toss the mixture into a hot pan.
8. Scatter over the pine nuts and Pecorino and serve immediately on preheated plates.

Nutrition Facts:
Garnished with tomatoes, pine nuts, and rockets, the light-filling meal provides many other vitamins and vital substances.

Nutritional values per serving:
Calories 579 | Fat 26g (Trans 0g) | Carbs 50g | Sugar 0g | Fiber 2,7g | Sodium 234,6mg | Potassium 769mg | Cholesterol 47mg

Active: 25 min ¬ **Total:** 30 min ¬ **Serving:** 2

SALMON SPINACH ROLLS

Whether on a buffet, the salmon and spinach rolls always cut a fine figure!

Ingredients:
- 2 eggs
- 8,4floz (248ml) milk (3.5% fat)
- 4,4oz (125g) wholemeal spelled flour
- 1 handful of mixed herbs (e.g., chives, parsley, dill)
- 7oz (198g) cream cheese
- 2,8oz (79g) baby spinach
- pepper from the grinder
- 4 tsp clarified butter
- 8,4oz (238g) smoked salmon
- pink peppercorns for garnish

Cooking:
1. Mix the milk with flour and salt until smooth, then stir in the eggs and leave the dough to rest for about 15 minutes.
2. Meanwhile, wash the herbs, shake them dry, and finely chop the leaves. Mix the cream cheese with the herbs. Wash the spinach, select, spin dry, and roughly chop.
3. Bake a total of 4 thin pancakes one after the other. To do this, heat 1 teaspoon of butter in a pan. Add 1 dollop of dough, sprinkle over a quarter of the spinach, and cook over medium-high heat 3-4 minutes on each side until golden. Use up the rest of the dough and spinach as well.
4. Use up the rest of the dough and spinach as well.
5. Place the pancakes on a cling film, carefully spread the cream cheese mixture, season with pepper, and place the smoked salmon on top.
6. Using the foil, roll up tightly into salmon rolls and chill in the refrigerator until ready to serve. Just before serving, cut into slanting slices, remove the foil, and garnish with pink pepper.

Nutrition Facts:

Salmon rolls also score points thanks to spinach with iron but also with folate (folic acid).

Nutritional values per serving:

Calories 516 | Fat 32g (Trans 0,1g) | Carbs 28g | Sugar 0g | Cholesterol 85,5mg | Fiber 8,5g | Sodium 398,8mg | Potassium 1026,5mg

Active: 20 min ¬ **Total:** 60 min ¬ **Serving:** 4

SESAME-CRUSTED SALMON AND BROCCOLI

Tender fish with an aromatic crust and crunchy vegetables

Ingredients:
- 1,3lb (590g) broccoli
- low sodium salt
- 1 clove of garlic
- ½ oz (14g) ginger
- 1lb (453g) very fresh salmon
- pepper
- 1oz (28g) sesame
- ½ oz (14g) coconut oil (1 tbsp)
- 2 tbsp sesame oil
- chili threads
- 1,7floz (48ml) vegetable broth
- 2 tbsp lime juice
- 1 lime

Cooking:
1. Prepare broccoli by cleaning and washing, boiling for 4 minutes, and draining. Chop garlic, grate ginger, and season salmon with salt, pepper, and sesame seeds.
2. Fry the salmon in coconut oil until golden, then bake in the oven at 100°C for 10 minutes.
3. Saute garlic, ginger, chili threads in sesame oil, stir-fry broccoli, deglaze with broth, and season with salt, pepper, and lime juice. Serve salmon and broccoli on four plates with lime wedges.

Nutrition Facts:

This dish contains Vitamin C, Healthy fats, Omega-3, and magnesium.

Nutritional values per serving:

Calories 393 | Fat 27g (Trans 0,2g) | Carbs 6g | Sugar 0g | Fiber 6,8g | Sodium 250,8mg | Potassium 955,7mg | Cholesterol 28mg

Active: 15 min ¬ **Total:** 30 min¬ **Serving:** 4

SALMON WITH BEANS, TOMATOES, AND VEGETABLES

Salmon with beans, tomato, and vegetables is a great source of protein and fiber.

Ingredients:
- 10½oz (398g) white beans (drained weight; can)
- 6 tomatoes
- 13,2oz (374g) fennel
- 1 clove of garlic
- 2 tbsp extra virgin olive oil
- 4,2floz (125ml) vegetable broth
- low sodium salt
- pepper
- 0,9lb (408g) salmon fillet
- 2 tbsp lemon juice
- 1 tbsp wholemeal wheat flour
- 1½ tsp fennel seeds
- 4 stems of dill
- 1 organic lemon

Cooking:
1. Drain, wash, and drain the beans. Scald the tomatoes in hot water, drain, rinse, skin, quarter, deseed and cut into small cubes.
2. Clean the fennel bulbs, wash and cut them into narrow strips
3. Saute garlic in oil over medium heat. Add fennel, beans, tomatoes, broth, salt, and pepper. Simmer for 5 minutes.
4. Rinse salmon and season with salt, pepper, lemon juice, and flour.
5. Fry salmon in oil over medium heat until golden brown. Add fennel seeds and simmer for 5 minutes. Meanwhile, wash the dill, shake it dry, and pluck off the tips. Rinse the lemon in hot water, pat dry, and cut it into wedges.
6. Arrange the vegetables and salmon fillets on 4 plates and garnish them with dill and lemon wedges.

Nutrition Facts:

This delicious recipe is a rich source of vitamins A, B, and C, calcium, potassium, and K.

Nutritional values per serving:

Calories 370 | Fat 17g (Trans 0g) | Carbs 22g | Sugar 0g | Cholesterol 65,2mg | Fiber 8,9g | Sodium 339,4mg | Potassium 1164,5mg

Active: 30 min ¬ **Total:** 40 min ¬ **Serving:** 4

MACKEREL FILLETS

Mackerel fillets on peppers and capers with bread. Deliciously roasted.

Ingredients:
- 2 red peppers
- 2 yellow peppers
- 1 red onion
- low sodium salt
- pepper
- 1,1lb (499g) mackerel fillet
- 7oz (198g) wholemeal bread (4 slices)
- 0,3oz (8,5g) parsley
- 2,1oz (59g) capers

Cooking:
1. Slice peppers and onion, and mix with olive oil, salt, and pepper.
2. Grill vegetables for 5-7 minutes, season, and keep warm.
3. Season mackerel fillets, and fry in remaining oil for 3-5 minutes per side. Toast bread slices for 2 minutes per side.
4. Top grilled vegetables with capers and parsley on bread slices, and place mackerel fillets on top.

Nutrition Facts:
Mackerel has a lot of omega-3 fatty acids, which have a very beneficial effect on the heart and blood vessels

Nutritional values per serving:
Calories 461 | Fat 24g (Trans 0g) | Carbs 31g | Sugar 0g | Fiber 0,2g | Sodium 90,2mg | Potassium 477,3mg | Cholesterol 64,5mg

Active: 10 min ¬ **Total:** 30 min ¬ **Serving:** 4

AVOCADO, ZUCCHINI, AND CHICKPEA HUMMUS

It is a perfect breakfast to warm up in the morning and will keep you sat until lunchtime.

Ingredients:
- 2 chopped courgettes
- 8-9 tablespoons tahini (preferably raw sesame)
- 1-2 avocados
- 8,8oz (249g) chickpeas
- 2 tablespoons nutritional yeast
- 1 lemon, its juice
- 2 garlic cloves
- sea salt (to taste)
- water and olive oil, if necessary

Cooking:
1. Mix all the ingredients in a blender until you get a homogeneous texture. If it is too thick, add water and olive oil until you get the desired texture.
2. Serve this hummus with sticks or little sticks, which you can prepare with celery, carrot, cucumber, or red pepper. Endives are also very good.

Nutrition Facts:
The cocoa provides a delicious chocolate flavor while also offering antioxidants. Blueberries are a rich source of vitamins, minerals, and antioxidants.

Nutritional values per serving:
Calories 327 | Fat 10g (Trans 0g) | Carbs 53g | Sugars 13g | Cholesterol 0g | Fiber 10,6g | Sodium 132,4mg | Potassium 345,8mg

Active: 10 min ¬ **Total:** 30 min ¬ **Serving:** 6-8

OATMEAL CHEESE PATTIES

Quick, easy, cheap, and delicious, even for non-vegetarians

Ingredients:
- 4 pork schnitzel or chicken,
- 1 onion
- 8,8oz (249g) oatmeal
- 7oz (198g) cheese, grated
- 8½ floz (251ml) milk
- 2 eggs
- low sodium salt and pepper
- paprika powder
- oil for frying

Cooking:
1. Chop the onion and combine it with the other ingredients. Add salt, pepper, and paprika powder to taste. Allow the mixture to sit and marinate for approximately 20 to 30 minutes.
2. Form meatballs and fry slowly in a pan with a little oil until brown.
3. Tip: Use tender or pithy oat flakes or a mixture of both. Leave the pithy ones a little longer, or add more breadcrumbs if necessary.

Nutrition Facts:
The recipe contains various micronutrients, such as vitamins and minerals.

Nutritional values per serving:
Calories 329 Kcal | Protein 6.1g | Fat 16.54g (Trans 0,1g) | Carbs 27.81g | Fiber 4,8g | Sodium 85,7mg | Potassium 261,4mg | Cholesterol 13,6mg

Active: 40 min ¬ **Total:** 60 min ¬ **Serving:** 6

HERB OMELET WITH SMOKED SALMON

The spicy treat is on the table quickly.

Ingredients:
- 1 cucumber
- low sodium salt
- 3,5oz (103g) smoked salmon
- 2 boxes cress
- 0,7oz (20g) dill (1 bunch)
- 6 eggs
- pepper
- 2,8oz (83g) kefir (4 tbsp)

Cooking:
1. Wash the cucumber and cut it diagonally into thin slices. Set aside a few cucumber slices, lay the rest flat on plates, and sprinkle with salt.
2. Dice the salmon. Cut the cress from the beds. Wash the dill, shake dry, and chop.
3. Whisk eggs with salt, pepper, mineral water, and kefir and stir in dill. Heat 2 tbsp oil in a pan. Add half the egg mixture and cook over low heat for 3-4 minutes to form an omelet. Fry a second omelet with the remaining egg mixture.
4. Top the omelets with diced salmon, cucumber slices, and cress, fold them up, cut them in half, and arrange them on the cucumber slices

Nutrition Facts:
The salmon scores with polyunsaturated fatty acids. Dill, the ancient kitchen and medicinal plant, has a mild nerve-soothing and antispasmodic effect.

Nutritional values per serving:
Calories 272 | Fat 21g (Trans 0g) | Carbs 5g | Sugar 0g | Fiber 2,5g | Sodium 347,5mg | Potassium 1026,7mg Cholesterol 24mg

Active: 15 min ¬ **Total:** 20 min ¬ **Serving:** 4

RECIPES FOR CAKES

BANANA, COCONUT, AND CHOCOLATE CAKE

Rich in fiber, it stimulates intestinal transit and is a good source of iron and phosphorus.

Ingredients:
- 2 bananas
- 2 eggs
- 1,4oz (41g) coconut flour
- 2½oz (74g) brown rice flour
- 1oz (28g) almond powder
- 1,4oz (41g) grated coconut
- 3,3floz (100 ml) vegetable milk
- 1oz (28g) coconut sugar
- 1 tsp baking soda
- 1 tsp cider vinegar
- 2 tbsp chocolate chips

Cooking:
1. Use a fork to mash the eggs.
2. Add the remaining ingredients and mix thoroughly. Alternatively, you may combine all the wet ingredients in a food processor and blend.
3. In a separate bowl, combine the dry ingredients.
4. Combine the two mixtures.
5. Bake for about 35 minutes in a greased pan.

Nutrition Facts:

Bananas, rich in antioxidants, is said to prevent the onset of many diseases. In addition, the sugars it contains help maintain good gastrointestinal health.

Nutritional values per serving:

Calories 327 | Fat 10g (Trans 0g) | Carbs 53g | Sugars 13g | Fiber 3,9g | Sodium 3,3mg | Potassium 438,2mg | Cholesterol 0mg

Active: 35 min ¬ **Total:** 60 min ¬ **Serving:** 2

CRANBERRY MUFFINS

A great classic of Anglo-Saxon pastries.

Ingredients:
- 5,3oz (150g) ground almonds
- 1,4oz (40g) brown rice flour
- 1,4oz (40g) buckwheat flour
- 6,7floz (198ml) vegetable milk
- 2 blueberries
- 2 tsp lemon juice
- 8 tsp maple syrup
- 1 tsp edible baking soda
- 1 tsp cider vinegar
- 1 pinch of low sodium salt

Cooking:
1. Preheat the oven to 180 degrees.
2. Mix everything and distribute the mixture between the muffin cups.
3. Add the blueberries.
4. Bake for 25 minutes.

Nutrition Facts:

This gluten-free, lactose-free, and refined sugar-free version has nothing to envy its competitors.

Nutritional values per serving:

Calories 144 cal | Fat 8g (Trans 0g) | Carbs 17g | Sugars 7g | Fiber 8,2g | Sodium 7,0mg | Potassium 265,3mg | Cholesterol 0mg

Active: 20 min ¬ **Total:** 50 min ¬ **Serving:** 2

BEAN BROWNIE

It is a great option for celiacs and people who have to eat gluten-free.

Ingredients:
- 8,8oz (249g) azuki beans
- 5,3oz (150g) of dark chocolate
- 2oz (57g) coconut or rapadura sugar
- 1,7oz (48g) coconut oil
- 1,4oz (40g) unsweetened cocoa powder
- 3 eggs
- 1 pinch of low sodium salt
- a good handful of pecans

Cooking:
1. Prepare the azuki beans beforehand: soak them for at least one night, then cook them for at least 45 minutes in unsalted water. Rinse and drain.
2. Melt the coconut oil.
3. Crush the Azuki and add the cocoa and salt. Mix well.
4. Add the eggs and the coconut oil-chocolate mixture.
5. Chop the pecans and add them to the dough. Leave some whole for decoration.
6. Pour into a greased dish, place a few whole walnuts on top, and bake for 25 to 30 minutes in the oven at 350°F/180°C.
7. Test cooking: If you like fondant, a knife blade should come out wet or with a little dough.

Nutrition Facts:

Azuki beans are easier to digest than other legumes. They contain large amounts of fiber, B vitamins (B1, B2, and B7), and minerals such as iron, manganese, magnesium, phosphorus, calcium, and zinc.

Nutritional values per serving:

Calories 350 cal | Fat 18g (Trans 0g) | Carbs 39g | Sugars 16g |Cholesterol 0g | Fiber 2,4g | Sodium 86,9mg | Potassium 153,5mg

Active: 90 min ¬ Total: 120 min ¬ Serving: 7

COCONUT CAKE

A delicious and very soft cake that will transport you to the islands

Ingredients:
- 4 eggs
- 1 cup coconut yogurt
- 2 tablespoons coconut sugar
- 2 tbsp melted coconut oil
- 2 jars grated coconut
- 2 jars brown rice flour in
- 1 tsp baking soda
- 1 tsp cider vinegar

Cooking:
1. Preheat the oven to 170 degrees.
2. Mix all ingredients.
3. Pour the preparation into a greased mold.
4. Bake for approximately 30 minutes.

Nutrition Facts:

This recipe contains high protein, healthy fats, Vitamin B12 and Vitamin D.

Nutritional values per serving:

Calories 270 cal | Fat 17g (Trans 0g) | Carbs 22g | Sugars 5g | Cholesterol 0mg | Fiber 9,5g | Sodium 6,4mg | Potassium 694,3mg

Active: 40 min ¬ Total: 50 min ¬ Serving: 2

CHRISTMAS GINGERBREAD

Gingerbread, also known as gingerbread, is a recipe deeply rooted in central and northern Europe and is served at Christmas.

Ingredients:
- 5,3oz (150g) honey
- 2oz (57g) brown rice flour
- 2oz (57g) Buckwheat flour
- 1,7oz (48g) Chestnut flour
- 1 cinnamon stick
- 1 tsp edible baking soda
- 1 tsp cider vinegar
- 1 pinch of low sodium salt

Cooking:
1. In a saucepan, boil the water with the honey, the 4 spices, the star anise, the salt, and the cinnamon.
2. Turn off the heat and let it instill covered for 10 minutes.
3. In a bowl, mix the flour and bicarbonate of soda.
4. Pass the infusion through a filter and pour it over the flour gradually.
5. Grease a mold and pour the preparation.
6. Place the mold on the Vitaliseur basket and cook for 50 minutes.
7. Once the cooking is finished, leave the cake inside the Vitaliseur for a few minutes.

Nutrition Facts:
Gluten-free and a good source of protein, fiber, and minerals such as copper and zinc.

Nutritional values per serving:
Calories 174 cal | Fat 1.2 g (Trans 0g) | Carbs 39 g | Sugars 20.7 g | Fiber 2g | Sodium 52,4mg | Potassium 85,3mg | Cholesterol 0mg

Active: 70 min ¬ **Total:** 110 min ¬ **Serving:** 2

BANANA WAFFLES

This one with plantains is always a real hit.

Ingredients:
- 2 eggs
- 2 bananas
- 2oz (57g) buckwheat flakes
- semi-brown rice flour
- 2,4oz (68g) ground hazelnuts
- 1,7oz (48g) apple compote
- 6floz (177ml) vegetable milk
- 1 tsp baking soda
- 1 tsp cider vinegar
- 1 tsp ground cinnamon

Cooking:
1. Mix the eggs, bananas, compote, milk, and vinegar in a food processor.
2. Add all the ingredients and mix.
3. Let the mixture rest for about ten minutes.
4. Scoop this mixture into the waffle maker.
5. Let them cook for more or less time as you like them more or less crunchy.

Nutrition Facts:
This recipe is a good source of dietary fiber and contains healthy fats from ground hazelnuts and vegetable milk, which provide essential fatty acids and other important nutrients.

Nutritional values per serving:
Calories 234 | Fat 11.4g (Trans 0g) | Carbs 26.5g | Sugar 8.8g | Cholesterol 0g | Fiber 6,2g | Sodium 2,4mg | 844,6mg

Active: 20 min ¬ **Total:** 30 min ¬ **Serving:** 2

OATMEAL CAKE IN BLENDER

It is a delicious, healthy, and perfect cake for breakfast or a snack in all seasons. The protagonist is a cereal rich in fiber and anti-inflammatory properties.

Ingredients:
- 2 cups rolled oats
- ½ cup wheat flour
- ¾ cup brown sugar (or stevia)
- 1 cup milk
- ½ cup neutral oil or lard or clarified butter
- 3 eggs
- 4 tbsp lemon zest
- 1 tsp vanilla extract
- 1 tsp baking powder

Cooking:
1. Put the oat flakes or flakes in the blender and blend very finely until it is the consistency of flour
2. Add the eggs, sugar, and milk
3. Add the wheat flour, the baking powder, the pinch of salt, and the lemon zest to the blender
4. Add neutral oil and vanilla extract. Blend again until you have a well-integrated mixture.
5. Grease and flour a 20 cm flan mold and pour the blended mixture over it,
6. Bake at 340°F/170°C for 45 minutes.

Nutrition Facts:
This recipe contains some vitamins and minerals from the ingredients used, such as iron from the wheat flour and calcium from the milk

Nutritional values per serving:
Calories 400 | Fat 19g (Trans 0g) | Carbs 53g | Sugars 30g | Fiber 5,1g | Sodium 43mg | Potassium 291,4mg | Cholesterol 0g

Active: 45 min ¬ **Total:** 55 min ¬ **Serving:** 6

EXTRA JUICY YOGURT CAKE

Yogurt cupcakes are one of my favorites. They're quick and easy to make, and they're great for kids' snacks.

Ingredients:
- 1 vegetable yogurt (in my case, coconut yogurt)
- 1 apple, peeled and cut into chunks
- ½ of the jar of coconut sugar yogurt
- 1 jar of chestnut flour
- 1 jar of almond powder
- 1 jar of tapioca starch
- 3 eggs
- ½ teaspoon baking soda
- ½ teaspoon cider vinegar

Cooking:
1. Preheat the oven to 350°F/180°C.
2. Use the yogurt jar to measure the rest of the ingredients and add them individually.
3. Place a sheet of baking paper in the bottom of a mold or grease it.
4. Pour the mixture into the mold.
5. Bake for 30-35 minutes.

Nutrition Facts:
Using coconut yogurt instead of dairy yogurt makes this recipe suitable for those following a vegan or dairy-free diet.

Nutritional values per serving:
Calories 343 | Fat 23g (Trans 0g) | Carbs 28g | Sugars 9g | Cholesterol 4,9mg Fiber 0g | Sodium 188,7mg | Potassium 634,5mg

Active: 40 min ¬ **Total:** 55 min ¬ **Serving:** 3

ALMOND CAKE

The almond cake is fluffy and tasty. To be served and enjoyed at the end of a meal, as a snack, for a nutritious, substantial, and energetic breakfast.

Ingredients:
- 10½oz (298g) almonds
- 5,3oz (150g) wholemeal flour
- 6,3oz (178g) brown sugar
- 5 eggs
- 2,8oz (57g) clarified butter
- 2½oz (71g) chocolate chips
- 1 lemon zest (grated)
- half a sachet of baking powder
- powdered sugar
- almonds to taste (to decorate)

Cooking:
1. Whisk the egg yolks and add sugar.
2. Add the melted butter, the sifted flour and baking powder, and the grated lemon zest. Mix well until you have a homogeneous and frothy mixture.
3. Whip the egg whites and add them to the mixture
4. Add the ground almonds and chocolate chips to the mixture.
5. Pour the batter into a pan. Bake at 180° for 45 minutes.

Nutrition Facts:
This recipe is rich in vitamins, calcium, and mineral salts; almonds contain omega-3 fats, which are useful for the proper functioning of the heart and beyond

Nutritional values per serving:
Calories 467 | Fat 30.3g (Trans 0g)| Carbs 40.4g | Sugars 25.9 g | Cholesterol 0g | Fiber 3,5g | Sodium 0,3mg | Potassium 207,8 mg

Active: 30 min ¬ **Total:** 70 min ¬ **Serving:** 5

COCONUT CHOCOLATE CAKE

Simple and quick to prepare; it is part of the sinless desserts. It is a light cake but full of energy!

Ingredients:
- 8,8oz (249g) of dark chocolate
- 1,7oz (48g) of coconut butter
- 2,7floz (80ml) of coconut milk
- 4,2oz (119g) of erythritol (if you use other sugar, increase the dose by at least 1,8oz/50g)
- 4 medium-sized eggs
- 2 tablespoons of potato starch
- 4 tablespoons of coconut flour (rapé coconut) + coconut garnish
- 1 teaspoon of baking powder

Cooking:
1. In a bain-marie, combine the chocolate and coconut butter and heat until melted.
2. After the chocolate has melted, mix in the coconut milk and sugar.
3. Add the eggs one by one, then the flour and yeast. Grease a pan, or use parchment paper, pour the mixture, and add the coconut as a garnish.
4. Bake at 180 degrees for 15/20 minutes.

Nutrition Facts:

High in antioxidants and can benefit heart health, cognitive function, and insulin sensitivity. It contains medium-chain triglycerides (MCTs), which can provide a quick energy source and may help with weight management.

Nutritional values per serving:

Calories 357 | Fat 26g (Trans 0g) | Carbs 28g | Sugars 12g | Cholesterol 0g | Fiber 10g | Sodium 57,4mg | Potassium 1281,7mg

Active: 20 min ¬ **Total:** 30 min ¬ **Serving:** 6

LEMON CAKE

Rich in vitamin C and thanks to its natural antioxidants, lemon stimulates the immune system.

Ingredients:
- 2 organic lemons
- 4 eggs
- 2,1oz (59g) brown rice flour
- 0,7oz (20g) arrowroot
- 2½oz (71g) of almond powder
- 1,4oz (40g) olive oil
- 1oz (28g) almond cream
- 2,8oz (79g) of brown sugar
- 1 teaspoon of poppy seeds
- ½ teaspoon edible baking soda
- ½ teaspoon cider vinegar

Cooking:
1. Mix the eggs and sugar.
2. Add the oil and almond cream.
3. Mix the dry ingredients except for the poppy seeds.
4. Grate the zest of the lemons and squeeze the juice from the lemon. Incorporate them into the previous mix.
5. Pour the dough into a previously greased mold
6. Bake for approximately 40 minutes at 175 degrees or steam it in the Vitaliseur de Marion for an hour.

Nutrition Facts:

It is excellent, among other things, for the hair, the liver, the skin, and the house.

Nutritional values per serving:

Calories 314 | Fat 19g (Trans 0g) | Carbs 30g | Sugars 20g | Cholesterol 0mg

Active: 45 min ¬ **Total:** 50 min ¬ **Serving:** 3

PLUM CAKE

This is a recipe for people living with endometriosis as it is a recipe with no inflammatory ingredients.

Ingredients:
- 5,3oz (150g) of almond flour
- 1,7oz (48g) of grated coconut flour
- 2 eggs
- 2 ripe bananas
- 1,7oz (48g) of coconut oil
- baking soda 1 tsp
- lemon juice 2 tsp

Cooking:
1. Beat the eggs and add the 2 ripe bananas previously mashed with a fork
2. add the coconut oil, the almond flour, and the grated coconut and mix well.
3. Add the level teaspoon of bicarbonate and two teaspoons of lemon juice. Line a mold with parchment paper and pour half the mixture into it, on which you can lay the apple slices, a nice puff of cinnamon
4. covered with the other half of the dough.
5. In the oven at 180° for 50 minutes if static and 40 minutes if ventilated.

Nutrition Facts:
This dish contains healthy ingredients such as almond flour and coconut flour, rich in fiber, protein, and healthy fats.

Nutritional values per serving:
Calories 263 | Fat 20g (Trans 0g) | Carbs 18g | Sugars 7g | Cholesterol 0g | Fiber 9,5g | Sodium 110,8mg | Potassium 694,3mg

Active: 50 min ¬ **Total:** 60 min ¬ **Serving:** 3

APPLE CAKE

This recipe is super simple, and the result is amazing. It is light, smooth, and very tasty.

Ingredients:
- 3-4 apples
- 3 eggs
- 1,7oz (48g) rapadura or coconut sugar
- 2,8oz (79g) ground almonds
- 1,4oz (40g) brown rice flour
- 1,4oz (40g) buckwheat flour
- 1,7oz (48g) olive or coconut oil
- 1,4oz (40g) whole almond puree
- 3,4floz (100 ml) of vegetable milk
- 1 teaspoon of baking soda
- 1 tablespoon apple cider vinegar
- 1 pinch of low sodium salt
- cinnamon

Cooking:
1. The oven should be preheated to 180 degrees.
2. Combine the eggs and sugar in a glass.
3. Mix in the oil, almond cream, and vegetable, followed by the flour, bicarbonate, and vinegar.
4. Transfer the mixture to a mold and arrange the apple quarters on top, with the cuts facing up and placed next to each other.
5. Sprinkle cinnamon over the top.
6. Bake for 25-30 minutes.

Nutrition Facts:
This recipe contains rich dietary fiber, vitamin C, and antioxidants, which can support digestive health and boost immunity.

Nutritional values per serving:
Calories 327 | Fat 10g(Trans 0g) | Carbs 53g | Sugars 13g | Fiber 4,4g | Sodium 1,8mg | Potassium 194,7mg | Cholesterol 0mg

Active: 30 min ¬ **Total:** 40 min ¬ **Serving:** 3

BROCCOLI AND SALMON CAKE

Accompanied by salad, this healthy, easy, and complete recipe will delight everyone.

Ingredients:
- ½ cooked broccoli
- 4,2oz (119g) of smoked salmon
- 3 eggs
- 1 tbsp of vegetable milk
- 1,7oz (48g) chickpea flour
- 1,7oz (48g) brown rice flour
- ½ teaspoon bicarbonate of soda
- ½ teaspoon cider vinegar

Cooking:
1. Preheat the oven to 180 degrees.
2. Beat the eggs.
3. Add, in order, flour, yeast, oil, and milk.
4. Add the salmon, broccoli, curry, and turmeric. Add the salt and pepper.
5. Pour the mixture into a cake pan.
6. Bake for 45 min.

Nutrition Facts:
Excellent source of nutrients, broccoli contains vitamins C, K, E, and B9, which are essential for health. It is food particularly rich in sulfur, magnesium, calcium, and potassium

Nutritional values per serving:
Calories 269 | Fat 11.3g | Carbs 21.9g | Sugars 2.6g | Cholesterol 28mg | Fiber 6,8g | Sodium 1412,6mg | Potassium 944,7mg

Active: 45 min ¬ **Total:** 55 min ¬ **Serving:** 3

SNACK RECIPES

BANANA OATMEAL MUFFINS

Breakfast muffins are convenient, easy, and a great way to use overripe bananas. They add sweetness to this recipe, so there is no added sugar.

Ingredients:
- ½ cup oatmeal
- 1 cup instant oatmeal
- 1 st. l. baking powder
- ½ tsp baking soda
- ½ tsp low sodium salt
- 3 large bananas, mashed
- 2 large eggs, lightly beaten
- ⅓ cup extra virgin olive oil

Cooking:
1. Preheat the oven to 190 degrees. Arrange paper liners in a cupcake pan.
2. Mix oatmeal, baking powder, baking soda, and salt in a medium bowl.
3. Add mashed bananas, eggs, and butter, and mix well. The dough will be thick.
4. Spread the batter evenly into the prepared paper liners.
5. Bake for 20-25 minutes; when lightly pressed, the finished muffin quickly restores its shape.

Nutrition Facts:
This recipe is a great source of fiber, which can promote satiety. It is also rich in minerals such as iron and magnesium.

Nutritional values per serving:
Calories 170 | Fats 9 g (Trans 0,2)| Carbs 21 g | Sugar 4 g | Fiber 12,6g | Sodium 121,5mg | Potassium 1021,6mg | Cholesterol 19,5mg

Active: 25 min ¬ **Total:** 35 min ¬ **Serving:** 2

TOAST WITH CHICKPEA PASTE, AVOCADO, AND TOMATOES

This recipe tastes avocado toast to a whole new level. This delicious, hearty, and healthy vegan Mediterranean dish will fill you up until lunchtime.

Ingredients:
- 2 slices whole grain bread
- 2 slices of tomato
- extra virgin olive oil for greasing bread and tomatoes
- ¼ cup chickpea or hummus paste
- ½ mashed avocado
- ¼ tsp sea salt
- ground black pepper to taste

Cooking:
1. toast the bread in the toaster.
2. While the bread is cooking, heat the grill rack or skillet.
3. Brush the tomato with olive oil. Grill each side for 1-2 minutes until characteristic stripes appear, and place them on a plate.
4. Once the bread is ready, brush it with olive oil. Spread the chickpea paste evenly. Top with mashed avocado, and garnish each piece with a slice of tomato.
5. Season with sea salt and ground black pepper and serve immediately.

Nutrition Facts:

This recipe contains more fiber, vitamins, and minerals. It can help regulate sugar levels and improve digestive health.

Nutritional values per serving:

Calories 220 | Fats 11g (Trans 0g) | Carbs 2 g | Sugar 2g |Fiber 11g | Sodium 363,2mg | Potassium 704,1mg | Cholesterol 0mg

Active: 5 min ¬ **Total:** 10 min ¬ **Serving:** 1

LENTIL RAGOUT WITH VEGETABLES

The stew usually takes hours, but this perfect dish for lunch or dinner is cooked in minutes.

Ingredients:
- 1 st. l. extra virgin olive oil
- 1 chopped onion
- 3 carrots, peeled and cut into slices
- 8 small brussels sprouts, cut in half
- 1 large turnip
- 1 garlic clove, sliced
- 6 cups vegetable broth
- 1 can (15oz/425 g) lentils, rinsed and pat dry
- 1 cup frozen corn
- 1 tsp low sodium salt
- ¼ tsp ground black pepper
- 1 st. l. fresh chopped parsley

Cooking:
1. Begin by heating the oil in a roaster over high heat. Once hot, add the onion and sauté lightly for about 3 minutes or until soft.
2. Next, add the carrots, Brussels sprouts, turnips, and garlic, and continue sauteing for 3 more minutes.
3. Pour in the broth and bring the mixture to a boil. Reduce the heat to a simmer and let the vegetables cook for about 5 minutes until tender.
4. Then, add the lentils, corn, salt, pepper, and parsley, and cook for another minute or so until the lentils and corn are warmed through.

Nutrition Facts:
This recipe contains healthy fats and antioxidants, which can improve heart health.

Nutritional values per serving:
Calories 240 | Fats 4g (trans 0g) | Carbs 42g | Sugar 11g | Cholesterol 0g | Fiber 5g | Sodium 410,2mg | Potassium 611,9mg

Active: 12 min ¬ **Total:** 15 min ¬ **Serving:** 4

TURKEY THIGH WITH MUSHROOMS

This dish combines turkey and mushrooms cooked in broth and wine. If you're not on any strict dietary restrictions, try serving the dish with one of the broad noodles and a generous helping of grated Parmesan.

Ingredients:
- 1 tsp extra virgin olive oil
- 2 turkey thighs
- 2 cups chopped champignons
- 1 large onion, sliced
- 1 chopped garlic clove
- 1 sprig rosemary
- 1 tsp low sodium salt
- ¼ tsp ground black pepper
- 2 cups chicken broth
- ½ cup dry red wine

Cooking:
1. Pour the olive oil into the multicooker bowl (in the stewing mode). Add turkey thighs, mushrooms, onion, garlic, rosemary sprig, salt, and pepper.
2. Pour in the chicken broth and wine. Cover and cook on high pressure for 4 hours.
3. Remove the rosemary sprig. Use a spoon to transfer the turkey thighs to a plate.
4. Separate the meat from the bones, mix it with mushrooms, and serve.

Nutrition Facts:

This healthy and nutritious recipe balances protein, fiber, healthy fats, and vitamins and minerals. It is low in carbohydrates and suitable for those following a low-carb or keto diet.

Nutritional values per serving:

Calories 280 | Fats 9g (Trans 0,1g)| Carbs 3 g | Sugar 1 g | Cholesterol 39,9mg | Fiber 1g | Sodium 196,1mg | Potassium 534,8mg

Active: 4 hours ¬ **Total:** 4 ½ hours ¬ **Serving:** 4

CARAMELIZED PEARS IN YOGURT

These sweet, cinnamon-flavored pears are simply delicious served on a bed of yogurt.

Ingredients:
- 4 pears, quartered, peeled, and core removed
- 2 tbsp honey
- 1 tsp ground cinnamon
- ⅛ tsp low sodium salt
- 2 cups plain yogurt
- ¼ cup chopped toasted pecans

Cooking:
1. Add oil, pears, honey, cinnamon, and salt, cover, and cook until the fruit is soft, 4 to 5 minutes.
2. Remove the lid and let it simmer for a couple more minutes to thicken it up

Nutrition Facts:
This recipe has numerous health benefits, such as reducing inflammation and improving blood sugar control.

Nutritional values per serving:
Calories 290 | Fats 11g (Trans 0g) | Carbs 41g | Sugar 30g | Cholesterol 15,8mg | Fiber 3,6g | Sodium 160mg | Potassium 180,9mg

Active: 5 min ¬ **Total:** 10 min ¬**Serving:** 4

ROASTED NUTS

If you want a tasty and healthy snack, check out this Roasted Nut Recipe. These delicious nuts are the perfect and highly nutritious snack for any occasion.

Ingredients:
- ½ cup (2,5oz/70g) almonds
- ½ cup (2,3oz/65 g) cashews
- ½ cup (1,8oz/50g) pecans
- ½ cup (2,1oz/60g) walnuts
- 1 tablespoon olive oil
- 1 teaspoon sea salt
- 1 teaspoon black pepper
- 1 teaspoon garlic powder
- 1 teaspoon paprika
- 1 teaspoon caraway
- 1 teaspoon chili powder

Cooking:
1. To prepare seasoned mixed nuts, start by preheating your oven to 350°F. Combine the mixed nuts with olive oil, ensuring they are evenly coated.
2. Mix sea salt, black pepper, garlic powder, paprika, cumin, and chili in a separate mixing bowl. Add the seasoning mixture to the bowl of nuts and stir well to coat.
3. Spread the seasoned nuts out in a single layer on a baking sheet. Bake in the oven for 10-15 minutes, until the nuts are golden brown and fragrant.
4. When done, remove the nuts from the oven and cool a few minutes before serving.

Nutrition Facts:
High in healthy fats, fiber, protein, vitamin E, magnesium, and calcium and contains antioxidant and anti-inflammatory effects.

Nutritional values per serving:
Calories 279.06 | Carbs 9.49g | Fat 25.8g (Trans 0g) | Sugar 1.84g | Fiber 0,6g | Sodium 2,1mg | Potassium 318,9mg | Cholesterol 0mg

Active: 15 min ¬ **Total:** 20 min ¬ **Serving:** 2

ENERGY BITES

A delicious and portable snack made from nuts, dates, and oats. These bites are packed with fiber, healthy fats, and protein and are perfect for sweet tooth recipients.

Ingredients:
- 2 cups (5,8oz/165g) oatmeal
- ½ cup (4,6oz/130g) peanut butter
- ⅓ cup (4oz/115g) honey
- ½ cup (3,2oz/90g) mini chocolate chips
- ½ cup (2,8oz/80g) flaxseed
- 1 teaspoon vanilla extract

Cooking:
1. Mix oatmeal, peanut butter, honey, mini chocolate chips, ground flax seed, and vanilla extract in a large bowl until thoroughly combined.
2. Form the mixture into individual balls, measuring 1-2 tablespoons each.
3. To add a finishing touch, you may choose to roll each ball in shredded coconut or chopped nuts.
4. Before serving, refrigerate for at least 30 minutes in a sealed container.

Nutrition Facts:

This recipe is high in fiber, and protein, making it a great option for a quick and nutritious snack or breakfast on the go.

Nutritional values per serving:

Calories 265.57 | Carbs 32.13g (Trans 0g) | Fat 13.32g | Sugar 16.84g | Cholesterol 0mg | Sodium 41,3mg | Fiber 6,6g | Potassium 451,9m

Active: 40 min ¬ **Total:** 45 min ¬ **Serving:** 5

CHIA SEED PUDDING

A creamy and nourishing pudding made from chia seeds and almond milk. This treat is rich in fiber, healthy fats, and antioxidants and can be made with your favorite toppings.

Ingredients:
- 1 cup (8,8oz/250g) almond milk
- ¼ cup (1,5o/43g) chia seeds
- 2 tablespoons maple optional syrup
- ½ teaspoon vanilla extract optional
- 1 tablespoon blueberry optional

Cooking:
1. In a bowl, combine unsweetened almond milk, chia seeds, honey or maple syrup (if using), and vanilla extract (if using).
2. Whisk the mixture until the chia seeds are evenly distributed.
3. Refrigerate the bowl for at least 2 hours or overnight.
4. Once the chia pudding has set, give it a good stir to break up any lumps.
5. Serve chia pudding in bowls or jars, topped with fresh fruit or nuts (if using).

Nutrition Facts:

This chia pudding recipe is a healthy and nutritious snack or breakfast option high in fiber, healthy fats, and essential vitamins and minerals.

Nutritional values per serving:

Calories 183.61 | Carbs 24.26g | Fat 8.17g (Trans 0g) | Sugar 12.97g | Fiber 10,2g | Sodium 45mg | Potassium 775mg | Cholesterol 0mg

Active: 20 min ¬ **Total:** 25 min ¬ **Serving:** 2

CINNAMON PARFAIT

A creamy and nourishing pudding made from chia seeds and almond milk. This treat is rich in fiber, healthy fats, and antioxidants and can be made with your favorite toppings.

Ingredients:
- 3 egg yolks
- 2½oz (71g) brown sugar
- 1 packet of vanilla sugar
- 8,4floz (248ml) cream
- 2 tsp cinnamon

Cooking:
1. Mix egg yolks with the sugar and vanilla in a bowl and beat until fluffy.
2. In the second bowl, whip the cream and cinnamon until stiff.
3. Then stir the two mixtures together with a spoon.
4. Fill the parfait into a suitable dish and put it in the freezer for about four to five hours. Stir occasionally so the mixture freezes evenly.

Nutrition Facts:
A good source of protein, vitamins A and D, and minerals such as selenium and phosphorus.

Nutritional values per serving:
Calories 295 | Fat 23g (Trans 0g) | Carbs 17g | Sugar 10g | Fiber 2,8g | Sodium 0,3mg | Potassium 11,2mg | Cholesterol 0mg

Active: 5 min ¬ **Total:** 5 min ¬ **Serving:** 2

VEGAN BLUEBERRY PIE

The vegan blueberry cake tastes especially good when fresh out of the oven and is still warm. You can serve it with vegan vanilla ice cream or vegan whipped cream.

Ingredients:
- 0,9lb (408g) wholemeal flour
- 7,7oz (218g) Sugar
- 1 pack vanilla sugar
- 1 pack cream of Tartar Baking Powder
- 16,2floz (479ml) oat milk
- 6,7floz (198ml) unflower oil
- 8,8oz (249g) blueberries

Cooking:
1. Combine flour, sugar, vanilla sugar, and cream of tartar in a large bowl.
2. Whisk together oat milk and sunflower oil, and gradually stir the mixture into the dry ingredients until you have a smooth batter.
3. Add blueberries to the batter and mix gently. Either fresh or frozen blueberries may be used.
4. Grease a cake pan with sunflower oil, and pour the batter into it. Bake for about 40 minutes in a preheated oven at 180 degrees, using top and bottom heat.
5. To test if it's ready, stick one skewer in its middle and if they come out clean, they're ready.

Nutrition Facts:
This dish is suitable for vegans or those who are lactose intolerant. Oat milk is a good source of carbohydrates, fiber, vitamins, and minerals.

Nutritional values per serving:
Calories 377 | Fat 12.7g (Trans 0g) | Carbs 63.5g | Sugars 31.7g | Cholesterol 0g | Fiber 14,1g | Sodium 86,5mg | Potassium 486,2mg

Active: 40 min¬ **Total:** 55 min¬ **Serving:** 3

ZUCCHINI FETA SKEWERS

These Zucchini Skewers are very much tasty. To be served and enjoyed at the end of a meal, as a snack, for a nutritious, substantial, and energetic breakfast.

Ingredients:
- 2 zucchini
- 1 pack of feta cheese, 7oz (198g)
- 1 tsp olive oil
- 1 garlic
- 2 onion
- low sodium salt and pepper

Cooking:
1. Wash and dry the zucchini. Using a vegetable peeler, peel off strips from top to bottom and set aside flat on a plate.
2. Cut the feta into cubes that fit the width of the zucchini strips and wrap them with the zucchini strips. Fix it with a toothpick.
3. Mix the oil, herbs, spices, garlic, and diced onion and pour over the skewers. Cover and leave for several hours or overnight.

Nutrition Facts:
High in fiber, vitamin C, and potassium and a healthy source of monounsaturated and polyunsaturated fats

Nutritional values per serving:
Calories 189 kcal | Fat 14.87g (Trans 0g) | Carbs 3.26g | Sugar 5g | Fiber 7,2g | Sodium 124,7mg | Potassium 1158,6mg | Cholesterol 11,1mg

Active: 30 min ¬ **Total:** 40 min ¬ **Serving:** 4

ANTI-AGING WEAPON WITH RASPBERRIES

This delicious raspberry smoothie contains antioxidants and anti-aging properties to keep you looking and feeling your best!

Ingredients:
- 5,3oz (150g) raspberries
- 2 tbsp brown sugar (or stevia)
- 2,6oz (74g) nonfat yogurt

Cooking:
1. Puree the raspberries (except for 2-3 pieces) with the sugar.
2. Pour half the raspberry puree into a glass, layer half the yogurt on top,
3. Add a second layer, and spread the remaining yogurt on the raspberry mousse.
4. Decorate with some mint leaves and the remaining raspberries.

Nutrition Facts:
Raspberries contain potent protective substances that can slow down skin aging. Combined with protein, the effect is enhanced.

Nutritional values per serving:
Calories cal 154| Carbs 28g| Fats 12g (Trans 0g) | Sugar 6.7g | Cholesterol 0mg | Fiber 6,2g | Sodium 0,7mg | Potassium 332,9mg

Active: 10 min ¬ **Total:** 10 min ¬ **Serving:** 1

ANTIOXIDANT-RICH CHOCOLATE SMOOTHIE BOWL

Indulge in a guilt-free and decadent treat with this antioxidant-rich chocolate smoothie bowl, topped with fresh fruits and nuts.

Ingredients:
- 1 frozen banana
- 1 tablespoon unsweetened cocoa powder
- 1 tablespoon almond butter
- ¼ cup unsweetened coconut milk
- 1 tablespoon of raw honey
- for the topping: grated coconut, blueberries, chia seeds

Cooking:
1. Place all the ingredients, minus the topping, in a blender and blend until smooth
2. Pour into a serving dish and top with topping of choice.

Nutrition Facts:
This dish is high in fiber, potassium, and healthy fats. It is a good source of antioxidants from cocoa powder, blueberries, and chia seeds.

Nutritional values per serving:
Calories 314 | Carbs 44g | Fat 14g Trans 0,1g) | Sugar 24g | Fiber 2,2g | Sodium 86,2mg | Potassium 1398mg | Cholesterol 15,1mg

Active: 5 min ¬ **Total:** 5 min ¬ **Serving:** 1

BANANA BREAD WITH CHIA SEEDS AND ALMOND MILK

This delicious banana bread is packed with nutrient-rich chia seeds and the subtle nuttiness of almond milk for a satisfyingly wholesome treat.

Ingredients:
- 2 large banana
- 4,2floz (124ml) almond milk
- 2 tbsp buttery soft
- 1 egg
- 4,2oz (119g) sugar brown
- 6,3oz (179g) lour
- 2 teaspoons baking powder
- ¼ tsp low sodium salt
- 3½ oz (99g) chia seeds

Cooking:
1. Preheat the oven to 390°F/200°C (top/bottom heat).
2. Mash the bananas with almond milk, butter, egg, and sugar using an immersion blender.
3. Add flour, salt, and baking powder, and fold in chia seeds.
4. Pour everything into the loaf pan and bake for 60 minutes.

Nutrition Facts:
This dish is a good fiber, protein, vitamins, and minerals source.

Nutritional values per serving:
Calories 271 | Carbs 47g | Fat 6g (Trans 0mg)| Sugar 19g | Cholesterol 0mg | Fiber 5,3g | Sodium 2,3mg | Potassium 542,1mg

Active: 20 min ¬ **Total:** 35 min ¬ **Serving:** 3

STRAWBERRY COLLAGEN GUMS

Satisfy your sweet tooth with these delicious, low-sugar strawberry collagen gummies that support healthy skin and joints.

Ingredients:
- 2 cups of fresh strawberries
- 1 cup unsweetened oat milk
- 1 tablespoon of raw honey
- 2 scoops of collagen peptides
- 2 tablespoons gelatin

Cooking:
1. Add the strawberries and milk you choose to a high-speed blender and puree until smooth.
2. Place the strawberry puree and remaining ingredients in a stockpot over low/medium heat and whisk well. Heat until the mixture is free of lumps.
3. Remove from heat and gently pour into mini silicone molds (there are so many different shapes you can find online, such as hearts, stars, or seasonally inspired shapes).
4. Place the gummy bears in the fridge for about an hour to harden before removing them from the molds.
5. Place it in the fridge.

Nutrition Facts:
This dish is a low-calorie, low-fat, and low-sugar treat that provides vitamins, minerals, and protein.

Nutritional values per serving:
Calories 280 | Carbs 35.7 g | Sugar 20g | Fats 1.3g (Trans 0g) | Fiber 2,1g | Sodium 1,4mg | Potassium 220,3mg | Cholesterol 0mg

Active: 10 min ¬ **Total:** 20 min ¬ **Serving:** 2

BEVERAGE RECIPES

PAPAYA SMOOTHIE

Enjoy papaya, and not just for its flavor. It is one of the fruits you should include in your anti-inflammatory diet due to its papain content.

Ingredients:
- 1 papaya
- 1 carrot
- ½ mango
- ½ banana
- 1 tablespoon pumpkin seeds
- 1 heaping tablespoon of yogurt
- ½ teaspoon turmeric
- ¾ cup orange juice

Cooking:
1. Put everything in a high-speed blender.
2. Beat to form a creamy mixture.
3. Serve with ice cubes or crushed ice.

Nutrition Facts:
The recipe contains a good amount of vitamins A, C, potassium, and calcium from the fruit and yogurt. It also provides some healthy fats and protein from pumpkin seeds.

Nutritional values per serving:
Calories 287 | Fat 8g (Trans 0g) | Carbs 53g | Sugar 35g | Cholesterol 0mg | Fiber 41,6g | Sodium 32,6mg | Potassium 2641,7mg

Active: 5 min ¬ **Total:** 5 min ¬ **Serving:** 3

GINGER TEA

Making ginger tea yourself is not witchcraft. For a cup of ginger tea, you only need a piece of organic ginger root - the slightly shriveled ones are usually hotter and, therefore, better suited for the tea.

Ingredients:
- ginger root
- 1 tablespoon of raw honey

Cooking:
1. Don't peel the ginger. Many important ingredients that make up the healthy effect of ginger are hidden in the peel.
2. Cut off a piece of the root, about 3 to 5 centimeters in size.
3. Put the ginger in a cup and pour hot water over it.
4. Let it sit covered for about ten minutes. Complete! Depending on your preference, you can sweeten it with honey or a vegan alternative.

Nutrition Facts:
The main ingredient of this recipe, ginger root, is known for its potential health benefits, such as anti-inflammatory and digestive properties. Raw honey is a natural sweetener with beneficial compounds like antioxidants and antibacterial properties.

Nutritional values per serving:
Calories 20 | Fat: 0g | Carbs: 5g | Sugar 5g Cholesterol 0mg | Fiber 0,9g | Sodium 48,8mg | Potassium 105,3mg

Active: 5 min ¬ **Total:** 7 min ¬ **Serving:** 1

SLOE JUICE

Sloe juice is fruity and healthy. It is said to have a positive effect on the immune system, stomach, and intestines.

Ingredients:
- 1 papaya
- 1 carrot
- ½ mango
- ½ banana
- a one-inch piece of ginger
- 1 tablespoon pumpkin seeds
- 1 heaping tablespoon of yogurt
- ½ teaspoon turmeric
- ¾ cup orange juice

Cooking:
1. Put all the ingredients in a high-speed blender.
2. Beat until a creamy mixture is left.
3. Serve with ice cubes or crushed ice.

Nutrition Facts:

This recipe contains vitamins and minerals, especially vitamins A and C, from papaya, carrot, mango, and orange juice.

Nutritional values per serving:

Calories 307 | Fat 9g (Trans 0g) | Carbs 55g | Sugar 35g | Fiber 6,9g | Sodium 90,3mg | Potassium 1456,4mg | Cholesterol 0mg

Active: 5 min ¬ **Total:** 5 min ¬ **Serving:** 3

ICE-MATCHA

Cool off and indulge in the refreshing blend of delicate matcha flavor and creamy sweetness with every spoonful of our delightful Ice-Matcha dessert.

Ingredients:
- matcha - 5 tsp;
- vegetable milk (oat, almond, soy) – 16,9floz (0.5l);
- Ice - 2 cups.

Cooking:
1. Pour the matcha into 8,45floz (250ml) of milk.
2. Beat thoroughly with a fork or whisk until the powder is completely dissolved.
3. Pour into a pitcher and add the rest of the milk.
4. Then we put ice in a jug - and the vitamin drink is ready!

Nutrition Facts:

Matcha lowers cholesterol levels, increases energy, and improves concentration. Rich in iron, calcium, and potassium

Nutritional values per serving:

Calories 175 | Fat 6g (Trans 0g) | Carbs 24g | Sugar 11g | Fiber 0,8g | Sodium 112,8mg | Potassium 457,8mg | Cholesterol 0mg

Active: 3 min ¬ **Total:** 5 min ¬ **Serving:** 1

COLD ROSEHIP AND RASPBERRY DRINK

Quench your thirst and delight your senses with the refreshing fusion of sweet raspberries and tangy rosehips in every sip of our Cold Rosehip and Raspberry Drink.

Ingredients:
- 1,7oz (48g) frozen raspberries
- 1,7oz (48g) wild dried rose

Cooking:
1. Pour boiling water over the berries, cover them, and leave for 15-20 minutes. The drink can be drunk both hot and chilled.

Nutrition Facts:
It is a storehouse of vitamin C necessary for supporting immunity and collagen synthesis. In addition, rose hip helps to get rid of edema.

Nutritional values per serving:
Calories 12 | Carbs 3 g | Fat 0.1 g | Sugar 1.5 g | Cholesterol 0mg | Fiber 4g | Sodium 5,4mg | Potassium 287,9mg

Active: 15 min ¬ **Total:** 20 min ¬ **Serving:** 2

CRANBERRY JUICE

Sip on the tangy and refreshing antioxidants with every sip of our deliciously tart Cranberry Juice.

Ingredients:
- 10½oz (298g) frozen cranberries
- Water – 50,7floz (1.5l);
- honey - to taste

Cooking:
1. Rub the lingonberries through a sieve, leaving only the cake in it.
2. Pour water through it, gently squeezing the skins of the berries with a spoon.
3. Water can be warm or cold - according to your taste. Stir the resulting drink thoroughly. If desired, you can add honey.

Nutrition Facts:
Cranberry juice has anti-inflammatory and diuretic effects

Nutritional values per serving:
Calories 126 | Carbs 32.5g | Fat 0.5g (Trans 0g) | Sugar 23 g | Cholesterol 0mg | Fiber 8,2g | Sodium 7mg | Potassium 265,3mg

Active: 5 min ¬ **Total:** 5 min ¬ **Serving:** 1

WHEATGRASS AND PINEAPPLE SHOT

This Wheatgrass and Pineapple Shot packs a nutritional punch with its high fiber content and abundant vitamins and minerals from the wheatgrass and pineapple.

Ingredients:
- 1,4oz (40g) wheat germ juice
- 6oz (170g) fresh pineapple juice
- Ice - 2 cubes;
- fresh mint - 3 leaves.

Cooking:
1. Squeezing the juice from pineapple. Mix it with wheat germ juice. Add ice and mint leaves

Nutrition Facts:
These low-calorie drinks are ideal for people who are trying to lose weight.

Nutritional values per serving:
Calories 66 kcal | Carbs 16g | Fat 0.4g | Sugar 10g | Cholesterol 0mg | Fiber 2,4g | Sodium 2,7mg | Potassium 181mg

Active: 3 min ¬ **Total:** 3 min ¬ **Serving:** 1

FLAXSEED AND DANDELION SMOOTHIE

Nutty goodness of Flaxseed and Dandelion Smoothie, a high-fiber and protein-rich beverage abundant in vitamins and minerals.

Ingredients:
- 0,4oz (11g) protein powder
- dandelion greens 3 leaves
- 0,2 oz (5,7g) cocoa powder
- ¼ avocado
- 10½oz (298g) coconut milk

Nutrition Facts:

Seeds are considered a source of fatty acids, and dandelion leaves have a beneficial effect on skin detoxification processes

Cooking:
1. Put all the ingredients in a blender or shaker.
2. In a blender or shaker, combine all ingredients.

Nutritional values per serving:

Calories: 308 | Carbs 11 g | Fat 28 g | Sugar 1 g

Active: 5 min ¬ **Total:** 7 min ¬ **Serving:** 1

SMOOTHIE "GOLDEN MILK."

This Smoothie "Golden Milk" offers a delicious and nutritious blend of whole milk, almond oil, and turmeric, providing anti-inflammatory properties and essential nutrients in every sip.

Ingredients:
- 3,4floz (100ml) Whole milk
- 1 tbsp almond oil
- pinch of turmeric and honey

Nutrition Facts:

It rejuvenates, removes wrinkles, and helps maintain beauty.

Cooking:
1. Mix all ingredients and add a pinch of turmeric and honey to taste. You can diversify the taste with fruits.
2. Using a blender, prepare a cocktail.

Nutritional values per serving:

Calories 190 | Carbs g | Fat 16g (Trans 0mg) | Sugar 8g | Cholesterol 0mg | Fiber 3,5g | Sodium 0,3mg | Potassium 207,8mg

Active: 5 min ¬ **Total:** 7 min ¬ **Serving:** 1

COOKIES & CREAM KEFIR SHAKE

Similar to yogurt, kefir is a fermented drink that's high in gut-boosting probiotics

Ingredients:
- ½ cup plain kefir
- ½ cup oat milk
- 1 frozen banana
- 1 tablespoon of unsweetened cacao nibs
- 1 scoop of protein powder cookies

Cooking:
1. Place all ingredients in a high-speed blender until smooth.

Nutrition Facts:

It offers a great protein, fiber, and healthy fats source while providing significant potassium, calcium, and iron.

Nutritional values per serving:

Calories 425 | Carbs 57g | Fat 12g (trans 0g) | Sugar 32g | fiber 4,8g | sodium 56,7mg | Potassium 1188,6mg | Cholesterol 10mg

Active: 2 min ¬ **Total:** 5 min ¬ **Serving:** 1

SALAD RECIPES

CHARD SALAD

The regional summer vegetable chard is versatile, aromatic, and also very tasty as a salad.

Ingredients:
- 1 chard
- 1 clove of garlic
- 2 tbsp olive oil
- 2 tablespoons white balsamic vinegar
- ½ tsp mustard
- 1 handful of walnuts, roughly chopped
- 13½oz (382g) cherry tomatoes
- some parmesan

Cooking:
1. Cut and trim the chard. Then blanch it in hot water.
2. If you want to prepare a warm salad, set it aside. However, if you prefer cold chard salad, rinse the blanched chard pieces with cold water.
3. Then put them in a salad bowl.
4. Mix the dressing by crushing the garlic, filling it in a screw-top jar, and adding mustard, oil, and vinegar.
5. Mix everything well and transfer them over the chard into the bowl.
6. Mix everything well and let it sit for about an hour.
7. Then add the chopped walnuts, chop the tomatoes, and chop the Parmesan and put these two ingredients to the chard in the salad bowl.

Nutrition Facts:

It is a healthy and nutritious option. This recipe is low in calories and high in vitamins A and K.

Nutritional values per serving:

Calories 365 | Fat 32g (Trans 0g) | Carbs 13g | Sugar 4g | Cholesterol 0mg | Fiber 6,6g | Sodium 261,3mg | Potassium 876,8mg

Active: 10 min ¬ **Total:** 10 min ¬ **Serving:** 2

SAUERKRAUT SALAD

You can prepare sauerkraut salad either raw or cooked. Below we present a raw salad variant: When heated, the healthy lactic acid bacteria in the sauerkraut would be lost. Raw sauerkraut is, therefore, particularly healthy.

Ingredients:
- 8,8oz (249g) of sauerkraut
- 1 medium carrot
- 1 small apple
- 1 medium onion
- ½ bunch of parsley
- 2 tbsp olive oil
- 1 tbsp brown sugar (or stevia)

Cooking:
1. Drain the sauerkraut a little, then place it in a large bowl.
2. Finely grate the carrot and apple and add both to the sauerkraut.
3. Cut the onion into small cubes and add them to the bowl.
4. Finely chop th parsley and add it to the sauerkraut salad as well.
5. Finally, add the olive oil and sugar to the salad and mix well.
6. Season the sauerkraut salad with pepper and, if necessary, some salt. Be careful with the salt shaker: the sauerkraut is usually salty enough.

Nutrition Facts:

This sauerkraut salad recipe contains vitamins C, K, and fiber. The sauerkraut provides beneficial probiotics for gut health, while the carrots and apples provide natural sweetness and additional nutrients.

Nutritional values per serving:

Calories: 244 | Fat 14g (Trans 0,1g) | Carbs 28g | Sugar 18g | Fiber 8,1g | Sodium 22,6mg | Potassium 34,7mg | Cholesterol 7,6mg

Active: 5 min ¬ **Total:** 5 min ¬ **Serving:** 1

ARUGULA SALAD

A rocket salad is quick to prepare and a very popular appetizer. Its special aroma also makes it a great side dish.

Ingredients:
- 2,6oz (74g) arugula
- a handful of fresh basil
- 1 handful of cherry tomatoes
- helped a cucumber
- 1 ball of mozzarella
- 2 tbsp balsamic vinegar
- 2 tbsp olive oil
- a pinch of brown sugar (or stevia)
- low sodium salt and pepper

Cooking:
1. Wash the vegetables well. Then shake the arugula and basil well dry and roughly tear both into small pieces. Depending on your preference, you can cut off the slightly bitter ends of the rocket.
2. Halve the cucumber and then slice it as thinly as possible. You can cut the cherry tomatoes into quarters or halves, depending on size.
3. Drain the mozzarella and cut it.
4. Combine arugula, basil, tomatoes, cucumber, and mozzarella, and toss the ingredients thoroughly.
5. Mix vinegar, oil, and sugar in a small bowl for the dressing, then add it to the salad. Mix properly, and season with salt and pepper.

Nutrition Facts:
This salad is made primarily of vegetables, meaning it is low in calories and fiber. Arugula and basil are rich in vitamins A and K, while tomatoes and cucumber are good sources of vitamin C

Nutritional values per serving:
Calories: 290 | Fat 22g (Trans 0g) | Sugar 5g | Carbs 10g | Cholesterol 0mg | Fiber 1,1g | Sodium 9,8mg | Potassium 225,5mg

Active: 10 min ¬ **Total:** 10 min ¬ **Serving:** 1

WHITE CABBAGE SALAD

White cabbage is also called white cabbage. The winter vegetable is best known as fermented sauerkraut. However, you can also prepare the cabbage raw as a salad.

Ingredients:
- 1 small white cabbage
- 1 carrot
- 2 onions
- 1 tsp salt
- 4,2floz (124ml) vinegar
- 4,2floz (124ml) oil
- 3½ (99g) of brown sugar(optional)
- 1 tsp cumin
- pepper

Cooking:
1. Remove the outer leaves of the cabbage. Then wash it thoroughly.
2. Remove the stem and divide the head of the cabbage into four parts. Cut the cabbage into thin strips.
3. Wash and grate the carrot into small pieces.
4. Peel the onions and chop them finely.
5. Place the cabbage and carrots in a salad bowl.
6. Sprinkle with a teaspoon of salt and leave for 30 minutes. The salt pulls the water out of the vegetables. Squeeze the vegetable strips neatly and let the water drip off.
7. Put the cabbage and carrots into the bowl. And put onions.
8. Add vinegar and oil.
9. Season the salad with brown sugar, cumin, and pepper. Let it steep for another 15 minutes

Nutrition Facts:
White cabbage is healthy and contains many valuable ingredients, such as folic acid, minerals, and vitamins. It is in season from June to April and is also a good winter vegetable.

Nutritional values per serving:
Calories: 135 | Fat 46g (Trans 0g) | Carbs 20g | Sugar 8.9 g | Fiber 4,5g | Sodium 71,2mg | 314,4mg | Cholesterol 0mg

Active: 20 min ¬ **Total:** 30 min ¬ **Serving:** 2

KALE SALAD

Kale Salad is a fresh alternative to traditional boiled kale.

Ingredients:
- about six large kale leaves
- about four to five
- 1 onion
- 2 lemons
- 1- 2 tablespoons tahini
- olive oil
- low sodium salt
- agave syrup or maple syrup
- ½ can of cooked chickpeas
- ½ apple

Cooking:
1. Remove the stalk from the kale, wash the vegetables thoroughly, and chop them up.
2. Cut mushrooms into slices.
3. Dice the onion.
4. Briefly sweat the onion cubes with the mushrooms in a pan until the onion cubes become translucent.
5. Take a bowl and put the kale in it. Then, drizzle the juice of one lemon over the kale and steep it for ten minutes. This will soften the tough kale leaves and make them more palatable while the leaves are steeping; you can prepare the dressing for the kale salad. To do this, stir the tahini into the juice of the second lemon. Season the dressing with olive oil, salt, and some agave syrup.
6. Place the chickpeas in a colander, rinse, and drain.
7. Meanwhile, cut the apple into small pieces. Add the pieces to the bowl with the kale, chickpeas, and dressing.

Nutrition Facts:

Kale is a superfood because it contains essential vitamins and minerals like A, C, calcium, and potassium.

Nutritional values per serving:

Calories: 221 cal | Fat 10.2g (Trans 0g) | Carbs 28.3g | Sugar 7.8g | Cholesterol 0mg | Fiber 22,5 | Sodium 45,6mg | Potassium 176,6mg

Active: 10 min ¬ **Total:** 20 min ¬ **Serving:** 3

SPANISH SALAD

Spanish salad typically contains various healthy nutritional items such as strawberries, basil, avocado, and olives and can be a healthy source of fiber, vitamins, and minerals.

Ingredients:
- 4 cups of baby spinach
- 2 ½ cups strawberries
- 1 avocado sliced
- ½ cup chopped basil
- ½ cup toasted pistachios
- ¼ cup olive oil
- 2 tablespoons balsamic vinegar
- 1 clove garlic

Cooking:
1. Wash the spinach and dry it with kitchen paper.
2. Remove the stems and put them in a bowl.
3. Add the washed and cut strawberries, the sliced avocado, the chopped basil, and the pistachios.
4. Cover with a strawberry dressing. To do so, pass through the blender half a cup of strawberries, the oil, the vinegar, and a whole, peeled garlic clove. Beat until creamy, about a minute.

Nutrition Facts:

This salad is made up of anti-inflammatory ingredients such as spinach, avocado, which also contains potassium to prevent fluid retention, and strawberries.

Nutritional values per serving:

Calories 367 | Fat 58g (Trans 0g)| Sugar 2 g | Carbs 34g | Fiber 1,7g | Sodium 1058mg| Potassium 331,4mg | Cholesterol 24,1mg

Active: 7 min ¬ **Total:** 7 min ¬ **Serving:** 4

SALAD WITH HONEY MUSHROOMS

It goes well with Italian dishes but can also be a meal with bacon and white bread.

Ingredients:
- 1,1lb (49g) mushrooms
- 6,7floz (198ml) orange juice, organic
- 1 large onion
- 2 garlic cloves
- olive oil and clarified butter
- low sodium salt and pepper
- 1,1lb (500g) lamb's lettuce
- 1 organic orange
- 7oz (198g) Parmesan in one piece
- balsamic vinegar

Cooking:
1. Make a sour salad dressing from chopped onion, balsamic vinegar, olive oil, and garlic cloves. Season with salt and pepper and other spices to your taste.
2. Peel the orange carefully. Reduce the orange juice to about ⅓ to ¼ of its volume.
3. Quarter the mushrooms and sauté in butter with oil, salt, and pepper. When ready, sprinkle a pinch of sugar over them and pour 2 - 3 tablespoons of honey into the pan. Now stir; the mushrooms should caramelize slightly.
4. Add the lettuce to the salad dressing and mix. Then spread the mushrooms "in heaps" on the salad and pour over the thickened orange juice. Place thin slices of orange on top. Finely grate plenty of Parmesan and place on top of the salad.

Nutrition Facts:
This recipe is rich in several vitamins and minerals, including vitamin C from the oranges, iron, and potassium from the mushrooms, and calcium and protein from the

Nutritional values per serving:
Calories 354 | Fat: 61g (Trans 0g) | Sugar 18g | Carbs 49g | Fiber 9g | Sodium 41,3mg | Potassium 429mg | Cholesterol 0mg

Active: 15 min ¬ **Total:** 35 min ¬ **Serving:** 2

SPROUT SPINACH SALAD WITH BEETROOT

This Sprout Spinach Salad with Beetroot is a nutritious and flavorful dish packed with antioxidants, fiber, healthy fats, and vitamins from various fruits, nuts, and seeds.

Ingredients:
- 4,2oz (119g) spinach sprouts
- 4,9oz (139g) beetroot
- 4,2oz (119g) blueberries
- ⅔ small mango
- 8 shelled walnuts
- 2 dates
- 2 tbsp sunflower seeds

Cooking:
1. Place the spinach sprouts, blueberries, mango, and beetroot cut into small pieces in a bowl. Add the date, nuts, and pipes.
2. Add the vinaigrette ingredients to a jar, close it, and shake it.
3. Dress the salad with the vinaigrette

Nutrition Facts:
This salad recipe contains various nutrient-dense ingredients such as spinach, beetroot, blueberries, mango, and walnuts. It is high in fiber, vitamins, minerals, and antioxidants, balancing healthy fats and carbohydrates.

Nutritional values per serving:
Calories 385 | Fat 22g (Trans 0g) | Sugar 31g | Carbs 43g | Cholesterol 0g | Fiber 3,8g | Sodium 173,6mg | Potassium 957,6mg

Active: 5 min ¬ **Total:** 5 min ¬ **Serving:** 1

SUPERFOOD SUPER SALAD

This superfood super salad is packed with nutrients and antioxidants from kale, spinach, blueberries, pineapple, parsley, mint, almonds, and pumpkin seeds, making it a delicious and healthy choice.

Ingredients:
- 8,8oz (249g) kale
- 2 handfuls of spinach
- 4,4oz (125g) blueberries
- half a small pineapple
- 1 bunch of parsley
- 1 bunch mint
- 2 handfuls of almonds
- 1 handful of pumpkin seeds
- juice of 1 lemon
- 2 tbsp extra virgin olive oil
- low sodium salt, freshly ground black pepper

Cooking:
1. Prepare your dressing. Peel the ginger and grate it on a fine grater. Squeeze out the juice from the lemon. Place all dressing ingredients in a screw-top jar and mix well.
2. Remove the tough core from the kale. Cut the kale into small pieces, and put them in a large bowl. Squeeze lemon juice over the kale, and mix. Add some salt, pepper, and olive oil. Rub the leaves with your hands for 1-2 minutes to make them softer.
3. Coarsely chop the mint and parsley leaves. Coarsely chop the almonds.
4. Peel off the skin of the pineapple and remove the eyes. Cut the pineapple in half lengthwise and cut out the tough core. Cut the pineapple into medium pieces.
5. Add spinach and greens to the bowl with kale, and mix. Add pineapple, blueberries, pumpkin seeds, and almonds. Pour dressing over salad and toss gently.

Nutrition Facts:
Foods such as kale, spinach, and blueberries are commonly called the buzzword superfood. This is because they reduce acidity, remove toxins, and have a powerful healing and anti-inflammatory effect.

Nutritional values per serving:
Calories 380.7 cal | Fats 32.7g (Trans 0g)| Carbohydrates 15.4g | Sugar 9 g | Fiber 8,8g | Sodium 6,4 | Potassium 1019,4mg | Cholesterol 0mg

Active: 15 min ¬ **Total:** 15 min ¬ **Serving:** 2

SIDE DISH

CREAM OF ASPARAGUS

It goes well with Italian dishes but can also be a meal with bacon and brown bread.

Ingredients:
- 0,8lb (363g) of fresh asparagus
- 1 small potato
- ½ small sweet onion
- ½ leek
- 20,2 floz (597ml) of vegetable broth
- olive oil
- low sodium alt and pepper

Cooking:
1. Remove the tips of the asparagus and reserve them for decorating the plate. Chop the rest of the asparagus.
2. Peel the onion and clean the leek. Finely chop them.
3. Pour a splash of oil into a pot and fry the onion and leek until translucent, about five minutes.
4. Peel the potato and crush it into pieces.
5. Put the potato and asparagus in the casserole.
6. Add the broth and cook everything together, for about fifteen minutes, on medium flame, until tender.
7. Shred the vegetables. If the cream has become a little thick, you can add a little more broth and, conversely, if it is too liquid, return it to the pot and cook until it thickens.
8. Put a little oil in a pan and grill the tips of the asparagus. Use them to decorate the cream.

Nutrition Facts:

A food that, in addition to being an important source of fiber, contains inulin, which reduces belly inflammation

Nutritional values per serving:

Calories: 160 | Fat 7g (Trans 0g) | Carbs 23g | Sugar 7g | Cholesterol 0mg | Fiber 2,5g | Sodium 41,1mg | Potassium 317,8mg

Active: 20 min ¬ **Total:** 30 min ¬ **Serving:** 2

STUFFED PINEAPPLE

Pineapple is a diuretic fruit, perfect for people who retain fluids and also for those who feel bloated since it contains elements that relieves digestive disorders and inflammation.

Ingredients:
- 1 frozen banana
- ¼ cup non-dairy milk
- ½ small avocado
- 2 handfuls of baby spinach
- ½ pineapple (to use as a container)
- ¾ cup fresh pineapple chunks
- 1 teaspoon flax seeds

Cooking:
1. Cut the pineapple in two and carefully empty the inside. Reserve the shell, as it will be the bowl for this dish.
2. Place the peeled frozen banana, milk, diced avocado, washed spines, pineapple chunks (leave a few for garnish), and flaxseeds into a blender or mixer and blend on high speed.
3. Pour the mixture into the pineapple peel when you get a creamy texture.
4. Decorate with raspberries, small pineapple pieces, coconut flakes, and pumpkin seeds.

Nutrition Facts:

This recipe is a nutrient-dense, refreshing smoothie bowl rich in vitamins and minerals. It contains healthy fats and fibers from avocado, flaxseeds, and antioxidants from spinach and pineapple.

Nutritional values per serving:

Calories: 330 | Fat 13g (Trans 0g) | Carbs 52g | Sugar 31g | Cholesterol 0mg | Fiber 7,6g | Sodium 27mg | Potassium 623,4mg

Active: 5 min ¬ **Total:** 5 min ¬ **Serving:** 2

ARUGULA PESTO

Arugula pesto goes well with many different dishes and is quick and easy to make yourself.

Ingredients:
- 2 bunches of fresh arugula
- 2,4oz (68g) nuts – pine nuts and walnuts
- 2 cloves of garlic
- 1,7oz (48g) Parmesan,
- 3,3floz (100ml) olive oil
- low sodium salt and pepper

Cooking:
1. Wash the rocket thoroughly and remove the coarse stalks if necessary: these are not as tasty but still contain valuable nutrients. Then place the arugula in a suitable container for pureeing.
2. Roast chopped nuts in the pan. Be careful not to burn them.
3. When the nuts are lightly roasted, immediately add them to the rocket.
4. Also, add the garlic to the bowl, breaking it up a little.
5. While you are now pureeing the ingredients, add the olive oil.
6. Finely grate the Parmesan and fold it into the mixture.
7. Finally, season the pesto with salt and pepper.

Nutrition Facts:

This recipe is a good source of vitamins A, and K. Nuts provide healthy fats and protein, and Parmesan cheese is a source of calcium.

Nutritional values per serving:

Calories: 150 | Fat 15g (Trans 0g) | Fiber 1,1g | Carbs: 45g | Sugar 7.9g | Sodium 9,8mg | Potassium 225,5mg | Cholesterol 0mg

Active: 10 min ¬ **Total:** 15 min ¬ **Serving:** 2

PEAR CHUTNEY

Pear chutney is a fruity and spicy topping for patties, tofu, and cheese.

Ingredients:
- 1 lemon
- 35,2oz (997g) of ripe pears
- 1 medium onion
- 1 small chili pepper
- 1 thumb-sized piece of ginger
- 1 sprig of rosemary
- lemon juice

Cooking:
1. Cut the pear, put them in a bowl, and sprinkle them with lemon juice.
2. Heat some oil in a saucepan and gently sauté the onions until translucent. Season them with two pinches of salt.
3. Add pear pieces, chili, ginger, and rosemary, and sauté for a few minutes.
4. Bring the pear chutney to a boil and simmer over low heat for about 45 minutes.
5. Let the chutney simmer until it contains almost no liquid and has a jam-like consistency. Season the pear chutney with vinegar and salt in between.

Nutrition Facts:
This recipe is a low-calorie, low-fat condiment rich in dietary fiber, vitamin C, and other important micro-nutrients.

Nutritional values per serving:
Calories: 300 | Fat 2g (Trans0g) | Carbs 280g | Sugar 17.5g | Cholesterol 5,8mg | Fiber 8,2g | Sodium 2,5mg | Potassium 308,9mg

Active: 20 min ¬ **Total:** 20 min ¬ **Serving:** 6

KKAKDUGI: RADISH KIMCHI

Kkakdugi is Korean-style fermented radish. The fermentation makes the root vegetable extra savory.

Ingredients:
- 2lb (907g) radish
- 1 tsp low sodium salt
- 4 Spring onions
- 0,7oz (20g) garlic
- 1 piece ginger
- 4 tbsp chili powder
- 1 tbsp soy sauce

Cooking:
1. Mix the radish with the salt and let everything stand for between 30 and 60 minutes.
2. Strain the radish and reserve the liquid.
3. Mix the radish with the spring onions, ginger, and garlic. Add the chili powder and soy sauce. If the mixture is too dry, add 2 tablespoons of the reserved radish liquid until it has a creamy consistency. Mix well.
4. Pour the mixture into a mason jar and press it together as compactly as possible. There should be no air bubbles left in the mass. Close the jar and let the kkakdugi ferment covered at room temperature for about five days.

Nutrition Facts:
Radish is a low-calorie vegetable rich in vitamin C, fiber, and potassium.

Nutritional values per serving:
Calories: 60 | Fat 0.4g (Trans 0g) | Fiber 35,9g | Carbs 13g | Sugar 7.5g | Sodium 639,8mg | Potassium 551mg | Cholesterol 0mg

Active: 60 min ¬ **Total:** 75 min ¬ **Serving:** 5

MEAL PLANNING TIPS AND TRICKS

LEARN HOW TO READ NUTRITION LABELS

An important part of following an anti-inflammatory diet plan is reading nutrition labels. To help you read nutrition labels for an anti-inflammatory diet, here are some steps to follow:

- Pay attention to the serving size: The first thing you should be aware of on a nutrition label is the portion size. This is important because all label nutrition information is based on this serving size.
  - Check the calories: Next, you should check the calories. It tells you how much energy you are getting out of your food.
  - Look for healthy fats: Anti-inflammatory diets emphasize healthy fats, such as omega-3 fatty acids, which can help reduce inflammation. Look for foods high in these healthy fats, such as salmon or avocado. Check the label.
  - Check for added sugars: Sugar can be a source of inflammation in the body. Look for foods with little or no added sugars.
- Check sodium levels: High sodium intake can also cause inflammation. So look for foods low in sodium.
  - Check for fiber: Fiber can help reduce inflammation in the body. So look for foods high in fiber. These include whole grains, fruits, and vegetables.
  - Look for anti-inflammatory ingredients: Look for ingredients such as turmeric, ginger, or garlic known to have anti-inflammatory properties.

If you follow these steps, you can easily read nutrition labels and make informed choices about your diet. Keep in mind that an anti-inflammatory diet is all about including a variety of whole, nutrient-dense foods in your diet and avoiding processed and inflammatory foods.

HOW TO PLAN MEALS IN ADVANCE

Meal planning is an excellent way to ensure you follow an anti-inflammatory diet. Here are some steps to help you plan your meals:

- Make a list of anti-inflammatory foods: Creating a list of anti-inflammatory foods is the first step in planning your meals. Foods high in omega-3 fatty acids, fiber, antioxidants, and phytochemicals should be included on this list. Examples include fatty fish/sardines/salmon, nuts/chia seeds, fruits and veggies/blueberries, kale, whole grains/brown rice/quinoa, and spice/turmeric.
  - Choose various foods: Variety is key when planning your meals. Try to include a variety of colors, textures, and flavors in each meal. This will ensure that you get a range of nutrients and antioxidants.
  - Plan your meals for the week: Once you have your list of anti-inflammatory foods, plan your weekly meals. Select recipes that include these foods and make a shopping list of the necessary ingredients.
  - Prepare meals: Set aside some time to prepare for the week once you have groceries. This might include cooking meals ahead of time, chopping vegetables, or making snacks. This will save time during the week and make sticking to your anti-inflammatory eating plan easier.
  - Consider your schedule: When planning your meals, keep your schedule in mind. Select recipes that are easy to prepare on busy nights, or that can be made ahead and heated.
  - Be flexible: Remember that it's okay to be flexible, even though meal planning is a tool to help you stick to your anti-inflammatory diet plan. Make adjustments to your plan if you feel like you need to make a particular recipe or if you have leftovers. Following these steps, you can successfully plan your meals for an anti-inflammatory diet. Remember to eat whole, nutritious foods and include color, texture, and taste in every meal.

HOW TO MAKE HEALTHY FOOD CHOICES WHEN EATING OUT

When you go out to eat, you probably have many concerns about healthy eating. Not being able to choose what to eat can cause stress and anxiety. But with these 17 ideas, you'll find it easier to stay on track with your diet.
What to eat | Weekend vs. Weekend Routine

There is a difference between Monday-Friday eating and weekend eating.
During the week, it is convenient to prepare a Tupperware to have better control of your intake. And if you need to eat out, you can follow these 17 ideas to help you stay on track.

How to manage your diet away from home:

Don't skip the snack
Do not skip your snack to control satiety, and avoid overeating when you go out for lunch or dinner.

Culinary preparations
Avoid eating high-energy foods, foods high in saturated or trans fats, and culinary preparations high in fat, such as fried, battered, or breaded.
If you have two meals, it is better to avoid dessert.

Watch out for starches
Do not mix starches; if you eat pasta or rice, do not eat bread.
If you must have bread, wait until it is served to eat it.

Vegetables for the first course or garnish
Different combinations of plant foods are available depending on the time of year. These will help you fill up quickly. Seasonal products are also their best price and ripening time. Salads, soups, cream, asparagus, and roasted vegetables are available. While fries may be the king of dining out, they are the easiest way to consume calories from fried fat. Better to have a vegetable side dish.
If it is a meal with a closed menu, have a snack before going to be able to avoid the starters that are usually very caloric (croquettes, empanadas, canapés, batters, doughs).
On special occasions, Christmas, family events, weddings, and cruises, the message is "moderation and common sense."

At fast food restaurants, choose a combo plate
Try to avoid them, but if they are unavoidable, choose vegetables for the main course and a salad with chicken strips or scrambled vegetables with fish. Always remember that vegetables should take up most of your plate.
Anti-inflammatory diet. Dish rule. Take care of your diet away from home.
If you go to a sandwich shop, choose whole wheat bread, try not to exceed 60 grams of bread, and fill it with vegetables with protein. Accompany the sandwich with an apple or other fruit or a handful of nuts.

Lightly cover. Dressings and condiments
We already know how good the tapas are; dare to try the less caloric ones: garlic shrimp, mushrooms, cured ham, and smoked salmon. Many will surprise you, and you can take care of your diet by enjoying delicious tapas.
Pickles and vegetables with dressings like bay leaf or thyme are more flavorful and filling. Choose your favorite spices, and when you eat out and have to watch your diet, ask them to add them to your dishes.

Aperitif
If you are going to have aperitifs, remember to drink only one or two glasses of beer or wine and always accompany them with a tapa which contains protein and is not very high in calories (Iberian ham, cured cheese, pickles, banderillas).
A 200 ml beer provides 90 kcal; if the beer is non-alcoholic, 34 kcal.

If you have eaten tapas or kebabs with a high caloric value, the next meal should be lighter, but you should never skip it. And try to exercise more.

Beverages

Drink a glass or two of water before eating to hydrate.

Take a bottle with you wherever you go, and fill it with cold or ice water and a few slices of lemon, orange, or cucumber.

Watch out for liquid calories

Sodas and commercial drinks are often loaded with hidden sugar. For comparison, a cola contains 35g of sugar, a chocolate shake 40g of sugar, and a healthy pineapple juice 42g of sugar per 330ml.

Watch your diet when eating out. Watch out for hidden sugars and liquid calories.

Watch out for alcohol

Be careful with alcoholic drinks. You add 100 calories to your diet every time you have a beer. If you're eating out and can't resist, limit yourself to one beer and always accompany it with protein.

Better tubular glass than a balloon glass

A Cornell University study showed that people who used tall glasses consumed less because they drank the contents more slowly.

Eat slowly

Eating slowly, chewing each bite slowly, makes you feel fuller and eat less.

Rest between courses

Also, support your silverware on the table between courses or while chatting.

The quick trick to overcoming temptation

If you feel very tempted by a particular dessert, the cake in the window, or your favorite ice cream in the corner, squeeze your hands together tightly. This focuses on that tension and distracts your attention from temptation.

Fill the refrigerator with fresh fruit or low-fat yogurt if you are staying in a hotel.

Those little refrigerators in hotel rooms hide unhealthy snacks when you want to eat well while traveling. So go to your local supermarket and pick up some fruit to snack on, along with low-fat cold cuts and nuts.

Win the battle of the all-you-can-eat buffet

When you find yourself surrounded by an abundance of delicious food you can eat in unlimited quantities, the best thing you can do is walk all over the place to discover the foods that suit you. Take your plate and divide it into 3 equal parts. Fill 2 of them with vegetables and the other with protein.

SHOPPING LIST

Following is the shopping list for an anti-inflammatory diet plan:

Fruits:
- Berries (blueberries, strawberries, raspberries)
- Citrus fruits (oranges, grapefruits, lemons)
- Apples
- Bananas
- Kiwi

Vegetables:
- Leafy greens (kale, spinach, collard greens)
- Broccoli
- Cauliflower
- Carrots
- Bell peppers
- Tomatoes
- Onions
- Garlic

Protein:
- Fatty fish (salmon, sardines)
- Lean poultry (chicken breast, turkey breast)
- Legumes (lentils, chickpeas, black beans)

- Nuts and seeds (walnuts, almonds, chia seeds)

Grains:
- Whole grain bread
- Brown rice
- Quinoa
- Oats

DAIRY ALTERNATIVES:
- Almond milk
- Coconut milk yogurt
- Healthy fats:
- Olive oil
- Avocado
- Nuts and seeds (walnuts, almonds, chia seeds)

- Spices and herbs:
- Turmeric
- Ginger
- Cinnamon
- Rosemary
- Thyme
- Basil
- Parsley

SUBSTITUTIONS:
- For dairy: soy or coconut milk, vegan cheese
- For gluten: quinoa, brown rice, gluten-free bread
- For meat: tofu, tempeh, seitan
- For the butter: olive oil, coconut oil, vegan butter

30- DAYS MEAL PLAN

The proposed 30-day meal plan is to be considered as an example and must be adapted in relation to one's physical constitution, gender, age, height and work activity, and lifestyle. For an overweight person, for example, a low-calorie diet is preferable. Therefore, the diet must always be personalized, taking into account the individual's and family's eating habits, as well as their relationship life needs, and it is therefore important to always seek the advice of an expert.

With the recipes in this cookbook, it is possible to obtain combinations that cover a food plan of at least 1500 days. Free your taste and imagination!

No. of Days	Breakfast	Lunch	Snack	Dinner
1.	Pumpkin and oatmeal pancakes	Tortellini Broccoli Casserole	Lentil Ragout With Vegetables	Potato Chicken Breast
2.	Mini Pear Crumble With Walnuts	Marinated Tofu	Roasted Nuts	Sesame-Crusted Salmon And Broccoli
3.	Granola bowl	Rutabaga And Mashed Potatoes	Strawberry Collagen Gums	Stewed Cucumbers With Salmon And Dill
4.	Mini Pear Crumble With Walnuts	Salmon Spinach Rolls	Zucchini Feta Skewers	Sesame-Crusted Salmon And Broccoli
5.	Oatmeal With Berries	Tarte Flambée With Beetroot	Banana Oatmeal Muffins	Salmon Spinach Pasta
6.	Mini Pear Crumble With Walnuts	Poke Bowl	Cinnamon Parfait	Salmon Meatballs On Leeks
7.	Blueberry Chia Pudding	Mackerel Fillets	Anti-Aging Weapon With Raspberries	Salmon With Beans, Tomatoes, And Vegetables
8.	Oatmeal And Cocoa Porridge	Oatmeal Cheese Patties	Banana Oatmeal Muffins	Tagliatelle And Marinated Salmon
9.	Blueberry Chia Pudding	Tomato Salmon	Caramelized Pears In Yogurt	Orange Salmon With Nut Rice
10.	Oatmeal And Cocoa Porridge	Oven Vegetables	Vegan Blueberry Pie	Lemony Fish Fillet With Zucchini Vegetables

11.	Granola bowl	Mackerel Fillets	Cinnamon Parfait	Trout Fillets
12.	Oatmeal With Berries	Vegetarian Meatballs	Energy Bites	Salmon Fillet With Peppers
13.	Mini Pear Crumble With Walnuts	Avocado, Zucchini, And Chickpea Hummus	Toast With Chickpea Paste, Avocado, And Tomatoes	Herb Omelet With Smoked Salmon
14.	Pumpkin and oatmeal pancakes	Salmon Spinach Rolls	Antioxidant-Rich Chocolate Smoothie Bowl	Sesame-Crusted Salmon And Broccoli
15.	Granola bowl	Mushroom pan with spinach	Chia Seed Pudding	Poke Bowl
16.	Oatmeal cookies and nuts	Vegetable Lentil Stew With Peas	Roasted Nuts	Vegetarian Chickpea Curry With Apricots
17.	Oatmeal And Cocoa Porridge	Cauliflower Steaks With Lentils	Caramelized Pears In Yogurt	Stuffed Salmon Trout Fillets
18.	Oatmeal and apple cookies	Vegetable Cakes	Lentil Ragout With Vegetables	Zucchini Lasagna
19.	Acai Bowl with Chocolate	Paprika Rice Pan With Yogurt Sauce	Turkey Thigh With Mushrooms	Pork Goulash
20.	Omelet with eggplant	Feta Cheese On Cauliflower Rice	Chia Seed Pudding	Mushroom And Zucchini Spaghetti
21.	Fluffy Artichoke Frittata	Stuffed Celery With Cheese	Energy Bites	Britta's Robber Meat
22.	Mini Pear Crumble With Walnuts	Avocado, Zucchini, And Chickpea Hummus	Toast With Chickpea Paste, Avocado, And Tomatoes	Herb Omelet With Smoked Salmon
23.	Coconut And Hemp Bars	Oven Gnocchi In A Tomato And Pepper Sauce	Banana Bread With Chia Seeds And Almond Milk	Salmon With Beans, Tomatoes, And Vegetables
24.	Acai Bowl with Chocolate	Cauliflower Potato Curry	Cinnamon Parfait	Tomato Salmon
25.	Porridge With	Meatballs Tuscany	Strawberry	Chili Con Tofu

	Golden Milk		Collagen Gums	
26.	Chia Pudding With Coconut And Turmeric	Salmon Spinach Rolls	Turkey Thigh With Mushrooms	Paprika Rice Pan With Yogurt Sauce
27.	Oatmeal And Cocoa Porridge	Casserole With Kohlrabi	Vegan Blueberry Pie	Mushroom And Zucchini Spaghetti
28.	Oatmeal cookies and nuts	Sausage Goulash And Minced Meat	Banana Bread With Chia Seeds And Almond Milk	Casserole With Kohlrabi
29.	Mini Pear Crumble With Walnuts	Zucchini-Spaghetti	Anti-Aging Weapon With Raspberries	Buckwheat timbale, peas, and tomato with sprouts
30.	Pumpkin and oatmeal pancakes	Casserole With Cabbage	Antioxidant-Rich Chocolate Smoothie Bowl	Chili Con Tofu

CONCLUSION

In conclusion, this cookbook is a labor of love that embodies our passion for culinary exploration and the joy of sharing delicious meals with others. Throughout these pages, we have strived to bring you a diverse collection of recipes that celebrate flavors from around the world while also providing a touch of familiarity with classic dishes.

Our journey in creating this cookbook has been fueled by the desire to inspire and empower both seasoned and aspiring home chefs. We firmly believe that cooking is an art form that allows us to express our creativity, and we hope these recipes serve as a canvas for your culinary masterpieces.

As you embark on culinary adventures with this cookbook, we encourage you to make each recipe your own. Feel free to tweak ingredients, adjust cooking times, and experiment with flavors to suit your unique palate. Cooking is an ever-evolving process, and we hope that this collection serves as a foundation for your culinary growth and experimentation.

We sincerely thank everyone who has supported us on this cookbook journey. From our dedicated team, who tirelessly tested and refined each recipe, to our families and friends, who provided unwavering encouragement and taste-testing assistance, this cookbook would not have been possible without you.

We also want to express our heartfelt appreciation to our readers, who have chosen to invite us into their kitchens and make our recipes a part of their dining experiences. Your enthusiasm and feedback have been invaluable, driving us to improve and expand our culinary offerings continuously.

In closing, we hope this cookbook becomes a well-worn companion in your kitchen, filled with stains and annotations that witness the memories and moments you've created with its recipes. May it inspire you to embrace the joy of cooking, discover new flavors, and, most importantly, cherish the simple pleasure of sharing a delicious meal with loved ones.

Happy cooking!

Wilhelmine P. Blake

AN IMPORTANT REQUEST

Dear reader, I am delighted that you have this cookbook. I hope you have at least a taste of the delicious recipes in this book.

At the end of my work, I have an essential request. Please give us honest feedback on our work. This will help us to improve the quality of our publications and to provide content that is increasingly tailored to the needs of our readers.

Tell us what you liked about the book, which recipes you liked best, or your suggestions for improving the cookbook.

Or maybe there are aspects of the book that could have been better. If so, your comments will be even more valuable to help us move forward and better meet the expectations of those who appreciate our work.

Please take a few minutes to write your sincere and honest personal review because your opinion is as valuable as your contribution to our improvement.

Thanks in advance for your time and consideration. Supporting and listening to our readers is what motivates us to improve continually.

My wish for you is a life full of well-being.

Wilhelmine P. Blake

© Copyright 2023v by Wilhelmine

Please read this Copyright statement carefully.

Reproduction, even partial, of the contents of this work is prohibited based on Title 17 of the United State Code, which dictates the principles of Copyright. All rights are reserved in all countries, including translation rights, electronic storage, and full or partial adaptation with any technology.

The respective authors own all copyrights not owned by the publisher.

The material provided here is general and is provided strictly for informative reasons. The information is presented without a contract or any warranty or promise.

This article aims to provide accurate and trustworthy on the subject and the problem addressed.

The publication is offered with the understanding that the publisher is not obligated to provide accounting services or other qualifying services that would be required official authorization. However, if legal or professional counsel is needed, a seasoned member of the profession should be contacted.

From a Declaration of Principles, two committees, one from The American Bar Association and the other from the publisher and associations, were accepted and endorsed equally.

The material presented here is claimed to be accurate and reliable, with the caveat that the recipient reader bears the sole and entire risk for any misuse or inattention caused by the use of any policies, practices, or instructions included within. Under no circumstances, whether directly or indirectly, will the publisher be held liable or responsible for any compensation, damages, or monetary loss resulting from the material included herein.

Printed in Great Britain
by Amazon